The Story of the American Legion

The History and Founding of the U.S. Veterans Organization in the Aftermath of World War One

By George Seay Wheat

PANTIANOS
CLASSICS

Published by Pantianos Classics

ISBN-13: 978-1-78987-244-6

First published in 1919

Contents

Foreword

The American Legion was conceived by practically the entire personnel of the army, navy, and marine corps! Every man in the military and naval establishment did not think of it in just such terms, but most of them knew that there would be a veterans' organization of some tremendous import, and here it is!

"A veterans' organization of some kind will be formed." I heard that identical remark not once, but a dozen times on board a transport en route to France as early as September, 1918. In fact, one night in the war zone a group of officers were huddled around a small piano trying to make the best of a lightless evening, and, having sung every song from *Keep the Home Fires Burning* to *You're in the Army Now*, paused, longingly toyed cigarettes which were taboo by ship's order, and then began to spin yarns.

"Reminds me of a G.A.R. reunion," one second lieutenant from Maine remarked, after a particularly daring training camp adventure had been recounted.

"Just think of the lying we'll all do at our reunions when this war is over," chirped a youngster from South Carolina. And then spoke a tall major from Illinois:

"The organization which you young fellows will join won't be any *liefest*—at least not for forty years. Don't forget there's some saving to do for the United States when this European mess is over. Us fellows won't ever get out of Uncle Sam's service."

How well the Illinois major hit the nail on the head! The incident on the transport seems worth recording not only because of the major but because it shows the general anticipation of what is now the American Legion. Perhaps it was this general anticipation which is responsible for the cordial reception that the Legion has had ever since its very inception in Paris.

No one can lay claim to originating the idea of a veterans' association, because it was a consensus among the men of the armed forces of our nation. A certain group of men can take unto themselves the credit for starting it, for getting the ball rolling, aiding its momentum, and, what is more important, for guiding it in the right direction, but no one man or group of men "thought up" the American Legion. It was the result of what might be called the "spontaneous opinion" of the army, navy, and marine corps caused by a fusing together in a common bond of the various elements of the service, just as spontaneous combustion is brought about by the joint action of certain chemical elements.

Spontaneous opinion, like spontaneous combustion, is dangerous when improperly handled and beneficent when rightly directed. That's what the organizers of the Legion have been and will be mostly concerned with. They have their elements—these men of the army, navy, and marine corps, and the organizers mean to direct this united and organized patriotism into such channels as will make for the welfare of the United States of America primarily, and, secondarily, for the welfare of the service men themselves.

Just how much attention this Legion with four million potential members intends to pay to the United States of America, and just how much to themselves *per se*, is basically important and pertinent as a question, nowadays when the Legion is being tried and is on the witness stand before public opinion. The answer is most clearly indicated by the preamble to the proposed constitution printed elsewhere.

This preamble stresses *Americanism, individual obligation* to the *community, state,* and *nation; battling with autocracy* both of the *classes* and *masses; right* the *master* of *might; peace* and *good will* on *earth; justice, freedom,* and *democracy*! Only in the last two words of the preamble is mention made of the welfare of the men themselves. These two words are *mutual helpfulness*. But be sure and understand the connection in which they are used.

"*... we associate ourselves together ... to consecrate and sanctify our comradeship by our devotion to mutual helpfulness.*"

This is the way the last purpose of the preamble reads.

The men who framed this constitution certainly did not believe that comradeship would be consecrated and sanctified by anything of a selfish character under the guise of mutual helpfulness. Certainly not the *comradeship* that made bearable the zero hour in the trenches or the watch in a submarine infested sea.

To go a little in advance of the story and speak practically, mutual helpfulness has meant so far voting down a pay grab from Congress; a get-together spirit to foster the growth of the Legion; a purpose to aid in the work of getting jobs for returning soldiers, and the establishment of legal departments throughout the country to help service men get back pay and allotments. Mutual helpfulness in this case would seem to make Uncle Sam as much a partner in it as are the Legion members. Because, for every job the Legion gets an unemployed man, and for every dollar Legion lawyers help collect for back pay and allotments, a better citizen is made. And better citizenship is what the Legion most wants.

So here seems to be the place to make the patent observation that *mutual helpfulness* will in future years mean just what it means today—doing something for the United States of America.

At the present time the Legion might be compared to a two-headed American eagle—one looking towards France and the A.E.F., and the other homewards to the service men here. The two are a single body borne on the same wings and nourished of the same strength. They are the same in ideal and purpose but directed for the moment by two different committees working together. One committee is the result of the caucus at Paris in March, when the A.E.F. started the organization, while the other was born this month in St. Louis, Mo., for the men here.

GEORGE S. WHEAT.
NEW YORK May, 1919.

Chapter One - Latter War Days in France

I believe that the army of to-day, when it goes back to citizen thinking and citizen acting, will be capable of so contributing to the commonwealth of the United States as to change the character of the whole country and lift it up to a higher plane.

BISHOP BRENT, *Senior Chaplain, A.E.F.*

Paris, March, 1919.

On a midsummer morning in 1918, ambulance after ambulance unloaded its cargo of wounded humanity at a base hospital in Paris. The wounded were being conveyed rapidly from the front and the entire hospital was astir with nurses, surgeons, and orderlies. A major, surgeon, almost staggered out of an operating room where he had been on duty for twenty-two hours and started for his quarters when a colonel arrived on an inspection trip.

"Pretty busy," remarked the colonel as he acknowledged the major's salute.

"Busy? Busy!" replied the major. "Good Lord, the only people about here that aren't busy are the dead ones. Even the wounded are busy planning to hobble around at conventions when the Big Show is over. Already they are talking about how they intend to take a hand in things after the war when they get home."

Over across the street a sergeant, limping slightly, stopped under a shade tree and leaned against it to rest. He was almost well of his wound and eagerly awaited the word that would send him to join his regiment, the Twenty-sixth United States Infantry. As he paused under the tree another soldier with a mending wound in the knee and just able to be about stopped to speak to him. The sergeant's hand rose in quick salute for the newcomer was an officer.

"Expect to get back soon, sergeant?" said the officer.

"Yes sir," he replied. "Anxious to go back and get the whole job over, sir."

"So am I," responded the officer. "But what will we all do when the Germans really are licked?"

"Go home and start a veterans' association for the good of the country, sir," the sergeant answered.

Lieutenant Colonel Theodore Roosevelt, then major, was the officer, and Sergeant William Patterson, later killed in action, was the enlisted man, and the institution was Base Hospital No. 2.

Colonel Roosevelt, who was in the hospital convalescing from a wound in his knee caused by a machine gun bullet, told me the story and said it was the first time that he had heard the subject of a veterans' association mentioned, although he had thought of it frequently himself as an organization with boundless possibilities for good. He found later that it was being very generally discussed by men in Base Hospital No. 2, particularly those who were so badly wounded that they could not be sent to the front again and who knew they must further serve their country along peaceful lines at home.

This was during war time, remember!

Then came the armistice!

When our victorious armies were wending their way towards the Rhine, when men of the navy and the marine corps realized that peace had come and that home was again within reach, this thought of a veterans' band, which had slumbered far back in the subconscious thoughts of all of them, burst into objectivity. An association of some sort was widely discussed not only by the men but by the officers as well. But how could even the start of it be begun? Those who considered the project most seriously were confronted with a difficulty which seemed at first to be almost insurmountable: that was the difficulty of assembling at one time and in one place a gathering which might at least approximately represent the whole army, navy, marine corps, or even the A.E.F.

This difficulty tended to narrow what is believed to have been the wish of everyone when he first thought of the matter, that is the hope that it would be another Grand Army of the Republic, another United Confederate Veterans, but greater than either because representative of a United Country. Talk started then about all sorts of imagined and fancied veteran organizations. Some advocated an officers' association. This was believed to be possible because officers had more freedom and more financial ability to attend a convention. Others thought the enlisted men should perfect organizations by regiments first, then divisions, and finally form one great united body.

The present leaders in the movement have since said that they realized that all of these schemes must come to naught because no organization except one on the broadest possible lines could be effective. They believed that all officers and men of the three branches of the service and all enlisted women, whether they served at home or abroad, should be eligible and urged to join one thoroughly democratic and comprehensive organization. They knew that any organization leaving out one or more elements composing the military service of the United States would be forced to compete constantly with the organization or association so discarded. In short, they knew that in union there is strength. And they believed, and still believe, that the problems of peace after a catastrophe such as was never before witnessed in history are so grave that they can be met with safety only by a national bulwark composed of the men who won the war, so closely knit, so tightly welded together in a common organization for the common good of all that no power of external or internal evil or aggression, no matter how allied or augmented, could hope even so much as to threaten our national existence, ambitions, aspirations, and pursuit of happiness, much less aim to destroy them.

Don't forget that the leaders of the movement realized all this, and also remember that they include among their number the enlisted man of the

A.E.F. and home army and the sailor in a shore station and on board a destroyer. The realization may not have been in so many words, but each knew he wanted to "make the world safe for democracy"—he had fought to do that and had thought out carefully what it meant, that is, that it didn't mean anything selfish—and each knew enough of the principle of union and strength to embrace the idea when "organize" first began to be mentioned.

But how to do it, that was the problem.

Then kind Fate in the shape of G.H.Q. came to the rescue with what proved to be the solution.

G.H.Q. didn't mean to find the solution. There had been a deal of dissatisfaction with the way certain things were going in the A.E.F. and on February 15, 1919, twenty National Guard and Reserve officers serving in the A.E.F., representing the S.O.S., ten infantry divisions, and several other organizations, were ordered to report in Paris. The purpose of this gathering was to have these officers confer with certain others of the Regular Army, including the heads of train supply and Intelligence Sections of the General Staff of G.H.Q., in regard to the betterment of conditions and development of contentment in the army in France.

Included in this number were Lieutenant Colonel Theodore Roosevelt, Jr., of the First Division, Lieutenant Colonel Franklin D'Olier of the S.O.S., and Lieutenant Colonel Eric Fisher Wood of the 88th Division. All of these officers have since told me that when they left their divisions they were distinctively permeated with the desire to form a veterans' organization of some comprehensive kind. When they got to Paris they immediately went into conference with the other officers on the questions involved in their official trip, details of which do not concern this story.

What is important is the fact that Colonel Roosevelt, Colonel D'Olier, and Colonel Wood each discovered that all of the officers in this representative gathering shared with the thousands of other soldiers of the American forces the hope and desire that the officers and men who were about to return to civilian life, after serving in the great war, whether at home or with the combat units or in the S.O.S., might sooner or later be united into one permanent national organization, similar in certain respects to the Grand Army of the Republic or the United Confederate Veterans and composed of all parties, all creeds, and all ranks, who wished to perpetuate American ideals and the relationship formed while in the military and national service.

When these officers realized what each was thinking they promptly set about with the "let's go" spirit of the A.E.F. to avail themselves of a God-given opportunity. A dinner was spread in the Allied Officers' Club, Rue Faubourg St. Honoré, on the night of February 16th and covers were laid for the following:

Lt. Col. Francis R. Appleton, Jr.,	2d Army.
Lt. Col. G. Edward Buxton,	82d Div.
Lt. Col. Bennett C. Clark, ex 35th Div.,	now with 88th Div.

Lt. Col. Ralph D. Cole,	37th Div.
Lt. Col. D.J. Davis, ex 28th Div.,	now att. G.H.Q.
Lt. Col. Franklin D'Olier,	Q.M., S.O.S.
Col. W.J. Donovan,	Rainbow Div.
Lt. Col. David M. Goodrich,	G.H.Q.
Maj. T.E. Gowenlock, ex 1st Div.,	now with 1st A.C.
Col. Thorndike Howe,	A.P.O. Dept.
Lt. Col. John Price Jackson,	Peace Commission
Maj. DeLancey Kountze,	G.H.Q.
Lt. Col. R.W. Llewellen,	28th Div.
Capt. Ogden Mills, ex 6th Div.,	now att. G.-2, S.O.S.
Lt. Col. Benjamin Moore,	82d Div.
Lt. Col. Theodore Roosevelt, Jr.,	1st Div.
Lt. Col. R.C. Stebbins,	3d A.C.
Maj. R.C. Stewart,	1st Div.
Lt. Col. George A. White, ex 41st Div.,	now att. G.H.Q.
Lt. Col. Eric Fisher Wood, ex 83d Div.,	now with 88th Div.

At that dinner the American Legion was born.

Why not let this gathering—the most representative in the history of the A.E.F.—consider itself as a temporary committee to launch the movement? Why not? everyone asked himself and his neighbor over the coffee. All felt that their presence in Paris presented an unusual opportunity to initiate the first steps of such a movement, an opportunity unlikely to be repeated and one they ought not to let slip. Another meeting was suggested to consider the matter. It was held. The result was that there were several more conferences and every such gathering was more enthusiastic than its predecessor. At each of these informal conferences, some one was careful to emphasize that these self-appointed committeemen were by no means representative enough of the army or navy, nor sufficiently numerous to warrant their actually effecting an organization of any character whatsoever. Yet it was believed that, nevertheless, the gathering was representative enough to act as a temporary committee so functioning as to get together from the whole army and navy two caucuses—one to represent the troops in France, and the other those who had remained in America and who, through no fault of their own, had been denied the privilege of making history on a European battlefield. The temporary committee realized that due care must be exercised in getting these caucuses started. Every unit in the A.E.F. should be represented, if possible, at the Paris caucus, while to the one in the States, preferably to be held at St. Louis because of its central location, delegates must come from every Congressional District in the Union.

Thereby would be avoided, it was urged, the mistake of giving the impression that it was a small gathering of men, unrepresentative or serving some special and selfish end.

This was unanimously agreed upon and the temporary committee elected Lt. Col. Roosevelt, temporary chairman, Lt. Col. Bennett C. Clark, temporary vice-chairman, Lt. Col. Wood, temporary secretary.

A sub-committee was appointed to receive from all the members of the temporary committee the names of such individuals of combat divisions and each section of the S.O.S. of the A.E.F., who were eligible and suitable to be delegates to a caucus scheduled for March 15th-16th-17th in Paris. A similar sub-committee was appointed to ascertain the names of men of the home forces in order that they might be urged to attend a caucus in America on or about May 8th-9th-10th.

The work of the sub-committee of the A.E.F. was much more difficult than would appear at first glance. It was easy enough to get the names of leaders in the various outfits, both of officers and men, but to get them to Paris! That was the job. Of course it was the ardent desire of everyone that the new organization should eventually become a society principally devoted to the interests of those who served as enlisted men, for they bore the brunt of the fighting and the work and were fundamentally responsible for the splendid victory.

But once the names of such men were in the committee's hands the real work had not begun. There were mechanical difficulties in securing for enlisted men in active duty leave to attend a caucus in Paris. In the first place the enlisted men themselves, as indicated by several who were consulted, were very diffident about accepting an invitation to attend a caucus where they would be required to sit beside and debate with and against generals and field officers to whom they owed military obedience. Then again, there was the expense of travel in France, as well as the high cost of living in Paris. At the outset this raised the expense of a trip to the French capital to a sum amounting to many months of an enlisted man's pay. Furthermore, the sub-committee was face to face with the A.E.F. regulations providing that except in the most unusual circumstances an enlisted man would not be granted leave except in company with a trainload of his fellows, and to a certain specified leave area.

But as has been said before the conclusion had been reached that if the organization was really to become preeminently an enlisted man's outfit, it would be absolutely necessary to overcome these difficulties and by hook or crook to obtain the attendance of as many privates and noncommissioned officers as possible who were leaders. So, scarcely had seventeen of the twenty officers returned to their commands before they received an urgent appeal to help out the sub-committee of three. They were told to get enlisted

11

delegates to Paris, never mind how, the method being of small importance provided the men were there.

Chapter Two - The Paris Caucus, March 15-17, 1919

The first delegates began to arrive for the caucus on March 14th. After-the-war good fellowship between those who had been commissioned officers on the one hand, and enlisted men on the other, was foreshadowed in a most interesting and striking manner when they began to come into the hotels. A dozen or more officer delegates brought with them as orderlies an equal number of delegates from the ranks. Thus enlisted personnel, by devious means, were ordered to Paris under one guise or another. One sergeant came under orders which stated that he was the bearer of important documents. He carried a despatch case wadded with waste paper. Another non-com., from a distant S.O.S. sector, had orders to report to Paris and obtain a supply of rat poison. Several wagoners, farriers, and buck privates acquired diseases of so peculiar a character that only Parisian physicians could treat them. As one of them said, he hadn't had so much fun since his office-boy days when a grandmother made a convenient demise every time Mathewson pitched. The expense of the trip was gathered in diverse ways. In some divisions the officer delegates took up collections to defray the expense of enlisted delegates.

In numerous instances, enlisted men refused such assistance and took up their own collections. One amusing story was told by an enlisted man. He said that the "buddies" in his regiment had deliberately lost money to him in gambling games when he refused to be a delegate because he couldn't pay his own expenses. So by various means nearly two hundred enlisted delegates were in Paris by late afternoon on March 14th. It must not be imagined from the foregoing that all the officers arrived on special trains and were themselves in the lap of luxury. One second lieutenant who attended has since confided that he sold his safety razor and two five-pound boxes of fudge sent from home in order to get carfare to Paris.

Practically all of the self-appointed, temporary committee, with the exception of Colonel Roosevelt, was present. He was Chairman of the American Committee and had left France for the purpose of organizing that part of the army and navy which did not get abroad or which had returned home.

The Paris caucus convened at the American Club near the Place de la Concorde on the afternoon of March 15th, Colonel Wood presiding. Lieutenant Colonel Bennett C. Clark of the 88th Division was selected Chairman of the caucus and Lt. Col. T.W. Miller of Pennsylvania, and serving in the 79th Division, was elected Vice-Chairman. When Colonel Wood called the meeting to order nearly one thousand delegates answered the roll-call and these were of all ranks from private to brigadier general; and every combat division and all sections of the S.O.S., were represented. Colonel Wood briefly reviewed the self-appointment of the temporary committee during the previous month and outlined the purposes of the caucus.

A few minutes after Colonel Clark had taken the chair an officer of high rank, a colonel to be exact, moved that while in the convention hall, the after-war status as fellow civilians be forecast and that the stations of rank would there cease to exist. It was agreed that they would be resumed with full force and full discipline as soon as the delegates crossed the threshold of the convention hall and regained the street.

It was the ability of the American officer to do this—to be friendly to a certain extent with his men and yet at the same time to keep them perfectly disciplined—which amazed the officers of the armies of our Allies. No more striking example of this was ever given than within the confines of the American Club on that 15th day of March. The Colonel's motion was unanimously carried and the work of the organization began. Then generals forgot their rank, corporals engaged in hot debates with colonels, sergeants argued with majors and everybody talked with everybody else in a most boylike spirit of fraternity and equality.

Captain Ogden Mills of G.H.Q. moved that four caucus committees be appointed to draft suggestions and submit them to the caucus, one committee to design machinery for convening the winter convention; one committee to submit suggestions as to a permanent organization; one committee on tentative constitution; and one committee on name. Each committee consisted of fifteen members, and was appointed by the Chairman.

Here are the committees, appointed by the chair:

Committee on Convention

Brig. Gen. Sherburne, 26th Div., Chairman

Wagoner Shaw, 88th Div., Vice-Chairman

Capt. Ogden Mills, G.H.Q.

Colonel Graham, S.O.S.

Prvt. C.W. Ney, 1st Army Troops

Captain Mahon, 77th Div.

Sgt. Obrecht, 1st Army

Capt. Kipling, Troops serving with French

Sgt. J.C. Hendler, Paris Command

Lt. Col. Appleton, 2d Army Hq.

Major Gordon, 36th Div.

Field Clerk Sowers, Press Section G.H.Q.

Major Hungerford,	3rd Army Hq.
Cpl. J.H. Anderson,	Paris Command
Lt. Col. Wren,	36th Division

Committee of Permanent Organization

Colonel Donovan,	42d Div., Chairman
Lt. Col. Graham,	88th Div., Vice-Chairman
Capt. Boyd,	29th Division
Sgt. Tip Bliss,	*Stars and Stripes*
Lt. Col. Fitzpatrick,	35th Division
Sgt. Rollo S. Thorpe,	88th Div.
Lt. Col. Crosby,	S.O.S.
Pvt. W.L. Thompson,	11th R.R. Engineers
Major Graff,	28th Division
Major Barry Wright,	79th Division
Sgt. Rommel,	Paris Command
Sgt. V.V. Trout,	Paris Command
Capt. Carlstrom,	S.O.S.
Major R.C. Patterson,	Peace Commission
Lt. Col. Smith,	89th Division

Committee on Name

Lt. Col. Robbins,	2d Army Hq. Chairman
Lt. Col. Goodrich,	G.H.Q., Vice-Chairman
Sgt. Dolan,	89th Division
Lt. Col. Stebbins,	3rd Army Corps
Sgt. H.E. Fleming,	35th Division
Major E.S. Haile,	77th Div.
Colonel Gibbs,	S.O.S.
Sgt. McElow,	Paris Command
Major Horace Rumsey,	35th Division
Sgt. C.E. Sommers,	Paris Command
Major D.D. Drain,	3d Army

Sgt. G.F. Fleming,	Paris Command
Lt. Markoe,	2d Army
Major Dwight,	S.O.S.
Sgt. Barnard,	Paris Command

Henry D. Lindsley
Temporary Chairman, who presided at St. Louis

The names of these committees are given because they are more than just names. They show the first bubbles of the melting pot into which all rank and titles in the American Army have been cast and out of which comes the one word "Comrade."

There were three outstanding features of the Paris caucus which were evident by midnight of March 15th. The first was the desire to get together and form an organization quickly and a willingness to forego personal prejudice and opinion to arrive at that end. The second was the determination to make the man who didn't get across as much a component part of the legion as his more fortunate brother-in-arms; while the third was the avowed intention to take no action at the caucus which could be deferred until the winter convention in America, when the home brother and the navy could be jointly represented and a permanent organization could be effected. I say that these things were evident by midnight of March 15th for those who have attended

15

many conventions know that from the casual word heard here and there, the whispered conference of a few leaders, and from the general tenor of discussions carried on by delegates gathered together in little groups, the spirit of the body politic is most perceptible.

After the adjournment of the afternoon session on that day, members of the committees closeted themselves and started work on their special functions, while those who were to pass on the committee's actions, the "hoi polloi" were here and there in groups, in the "Y" huts or in boulevard cafes discussing the real meaning of the gathering. A colonel in the Officers' Club said there must be no disagreement on this or that question; a private in the Bal Tabarin told his buddies the same thing.

And so it came to pass that on the following day in the Cirque de Paris, where the final meetings were held, the delegates formally gathered, sensed the gossip of the clubs and boulevards, and acted accordingly. One of the things done was to endorse the action of the temporary committee in appointing itself and in calling the caucus. Another was to adopt a tentative constitution. It is in reality little more than a preamble, but it gave a working basis, expressing enough and yet not too much.

Newspaper men have told me that the Sermon on the Mount is the finest bit of reporting in the history of writing because it tells a long story succinctly. Lieutenant Colonel Buxton and his committee on constitutions are certainly entitled to credit of the same type—for they tell a great deal in a few lines.

This gathering had no time for official photographers. A half hour before a session began one slipped in and took this picture with more than half the caucus delegates absent

Here's the tentative constitution under which the Legion worked—it was read by Lieutenant Colonel Bolles:

"We, the members of the Military and Naval Service of the United States of America in the great war, desiring to perpetuate the principles of Justice, Freedom, and Democracy for which we have fought, to inculcate the duty and obligation of the citizen to the State; to preserve the history and incidents of our participation in the war; and to cement the ties of comradeship formed in service, do propose to found and establish an association for the furtherance of the foregoing purposes:

"Those eligible to membership shall be: All officers and enlisted personnel in the Military and Naval Services of the United States of America at any time during the period from April 6, 1917, to November 11, 1918, inclusive; excepting however, persons leaving the service without an honorable discharge or persons who having been called into the service refused, failed, or attempted to evade the full performance of such service.

"The society shall consist of a national organization with subsidiary branches; one for each State, territory, and foreign possession of the United States as well as one in each foreign country where members of the national society may be resident and who desire to associate themselves together.

16

The Paris Caucus

17

"The officers of the society shall be a President, one or more Vice-Presidents, a Secretary, a Treasurer and a Board of Directors, which shall consist of the President, the Vice-Presidents, together with the chief executive of each subsidiary branch.

"The subsidiary branches shall organize and govern themselves in such manner as the membership of such subsidiary organizations shall determine upon except that the requirements and purposes of the permanent national constitution as adopted shall be complied with.

"The representation shall be on the basis of the actual enrollment in the subsidiary branches at all conventions after the adoption of a permanent constitution.

"Members present at the meeting of this committee as follows:

- "Lt. Col. G. Edward Buxton, Jr., Chairman
- "Lt. Col. T.W. Miller, Secretary
- "Major Redmond C. Stewart
- "Col. E.A. Gibbs
- "Lt. Col. W.H. Curtiss
- "Major J. Hall
- "Col. C.L. Ristine."

There were many, many men in the A.E.F. respected and beloved, but none perhaps more than he who seconded a motion made by a private from S.O.S. base section, No. 4, that the constitution be adopted. The seconder asked to speak on the question. When he began he got the rapt attention which Bishop Brent, Senior Chaplain of the A.E.F., always won whether he talked to buck privates knee deep in trench water or the King in Buckingham Palace.

"It was a great soldier who said that the army has not merely a body but a soul and a conscience as well," he began. "I believe the conscience of the army is speaking in this committee's report. I believe the army's soul is speaking in it. I was present on Saturday, at the beginning of this caucus and I will tell you frankly that I was fearful at that moment lest you should create a great mechanism without adequate purposes. My fears have been wholly allayed and I see in the report of your committee the ideals not only of the army but of the nation adequately expressed and I wish to tell you gentlemen that so far as I have any ability to promote this great movement I give you my most hearty support. I believe that the army of to-day, when it goes back to citizen thinking and citizen acting, will be capable of contributing to the commonwealth of the United States so as to change the character of the whole country and lift it up to a higher plane of political, industrial, and religious life. I happen to be at this moment leading in a movement in the army to promote the various ends that are so well expressed in the committee's report, in what is known as the 'Comrades in Service.' There are two ways of creating an organization; one is by forming the principles and leaving the body to take its own shape; the other by creating a machinery without stat-

18

ing your end and reach that end through the machinery. According to our democratic conception we have adopted the former or idealistic method. We are prepared to contribute to this army wide organization which is now brought into existence, all that we have to contribute. We are entirely loyal to your principles and methods of approach and we are quite willing to forego any attempt to make an organization which might become a rival to you. Between now and the time of demobilization there is a great opportunity for us to promote the principles which actuate you. We have already a temporary and provisional organization for the promotion of such principles; the creation of better citizenship along the lines so well expressed. We would like everyone who can to give support to that which we are endeavoring to do, while we ask all who come in with us to be prepared to throw in their lot with this organization when it is perfected in the United States."

"The creation of better citizenship," Bishop Brent says. He wants every one who can, to give support to that; to "what we are trying to do."

If everyone could see just that in the Legion, if everyone will work for just that—better citizenship—the Legion's aim will be realized in its deepest and truest sense. Bishop Brent has a knack of hitting the nail on the head with such force that the sparks fly and by their light comes insight—ask anyone from out Manila-way if it isn't so. The short address was greeted with thunderous applause. The newly born Legion knew it had a champion and a worker in the Bishop.

Col. Wm. J. Donovan of the 165th Infantry, Forty-second Division headed the committee of fifteen which gave the final report on resolutions and organization. This report is reproduced here in full because it presaged the action of the American caucus and brought about the form of the Legion Government until November.

"Resolved: That an Executive Committee shall be selected, two (2) from each unit (as recognized in this caucus) and eight (8) to be selected by the Executive Committee; the two members, one officer and one enlisted man, to be selected from each unit to be named by the respective delegations attending this caucus. Each unit shall present the names of committeemen who shall as far as possible represent, in point of residence, each State, Territory and possession of the United States and the District of Columbia.

"This Executive Committee shall have general power to represent the units now in foreign service, to determine its own quorum, to confer with committees from a similar caucus in the United States, to secure one general convention of persons entitled to membership under the tentative constitution, to elect its officers and appoint such sub-committees and give them such powers as may be proper and necessary.

"This Executive Committee acting in conjunction with the committee of the United States is specifically charged with the duty of fixing a date and place for holding a national convention, issuing a call for the holding of county and State conventions and providing a unit of representation and method of selection of delegates to the national convention, by the State conventions.

"The powers of this committee shall expire upon the organization of the permanent national convention.

"The committee is further charged with the duty of making known the existence and purpose of this organization, of stimulating interest in it, and of inviting the support of all those entitled to membership.

"No policy except in furtherance of the creation of a permanent organization having in mind the desirability of unity of action in organizing all the American forces shall be adopted or carried out by the committees.

A meeting for the temporary and preliminary organization of the Executive Committee shall be held at this place immediately upon the adjournment of this caucus.

The Executive Committee may receive and add to its number two representatives from any division or equivalent unit not represented at this caucus."

As the result of the passage of this report it is interesting to note the personnel of the Executive Committee which the delegates selected and which is controlling the American Legion of the A.E.F., observing especially the large number of enlisted men; large in view of the difficulties experienced in getting such men to Paris.

1st Div.,	Capt. Arthur S. Hyde
2d Div.,	Lt. Col Harold C. Snyder
26th Div.,	Sgt. Wheaton Freeman
26th Div.,	Lt. Col. Wm. J. Keville
27th Div.,	Lt. Col. Edward E. Gauche, N.Y.
27th Div.,	Reg. Sgt. Mjr. Samuel A. Ritchie, N.Y.
28th Div.,	Brig Gen. Wm. G. Brice, Jr., Penn.
28th Div.,	Sgt. Ted Myers, Penn.
29th Div.,	Lt. Col. Orison M. Hurd, N.J.
29th Div.,	Color Sgt. Andreas Z. Holley, Maryland
31st Div.,	Captain Leon Schwarz, Ala.
33d Div.,	Col. Milton A. Foreman, Ill.
35th Div.,	Lt. Col. B.C. Clark, Mo.
35th Div.,	Sgt. Fred Heney, Kans.
36th Div.,	Col. Chas. W. Nimon, Texas
36th Div.,	Sgt. Mjr. L.H. Evridge, Texas
41st Div.,	Col. Frank White, N. Dak.
42d Div.,	Col. Henry J. Reilly, Ill.
42d Div.,	Sgt. Rowe, Iowa

77th Div.,	Major Duncan Harris
77th Div.,	Sgt. Lawrence Miller, N.Y.
79th Div.,	Lt. Col. Stuart S. Janney, Md.
79th Div.,	Sgt. Benjamin R. Kauffman, Pa.
80th Div.,	Capt. Arthur F. Shaw, Mich.
81st Div.,	Major Theodore G. Tilghman, N.C.
81st Div.,	Reg. Sgt. Mjr. Wm. S. Beam, N.C.
82d Div.,	Capt. Frank S. Williams, Fla.
82d Div.,	Sgt. Alvin T. York, Tenn.
83d Div.,	Lt. Col. Wayman C. Lawrence, Jr., W. Va.
83d Div.,	Cpl. Thoyer
86th Div.,	Major John H. Smale, Ill.
88th Div.,	Lt. Col. George C. Parsons, Minn.
88th Div.,	Wagoner Dale J. Shaw, Iowa.
89th Div.,	Lt. Col. Frank Wilbur Smith, Pa.
91st Div.,	Lt. Col. John Guy Strohm, Oregon
91st Div.,	Sgt. Mjr. Hercovitz, Calif.
S.O.S. Hq.,	Col. James H. Graham, Conn.
Adv. Sec., S.O.S. Capt.	David A. Uaurier, Wash.
Base Sec. No. 1, S.O.S.,	Pvt. W.L. Thompson, N.Y.
Base Sec. No. 3, S.O.S.,	Lt. Col. Carle Abrams, Oregon
Base Sec. No. 5, S.O.S.,	Major Orlin Hudson, Kans.
Base Sec. No. 6, S.O.S.,	Major Arthur S. Dwight, N.Y.
Troops with French,	Sgt. L.K. Flynt, Mass.
Troops with French,	Capt. A.W. Kipling, Paris, France
Paris Command,	Pvt. Harold W. Ross, Calif.
Paris Command,	Lt. Col. John Price Jackson
G.H.Q.,	Bishop Charles H. Brent, N.Y.
1st Army Corps,	Lt. Col. Lemuel L. Bolles, Wash.
1st Army Corps,	Sgt. Mjr. Race
2d Army Hq.,	Lt. Col. Burke H. Sinclair, Colo.

The tentative name of this organization was not adopted without a great deal of discussion. All sorts of titles were suggested to the committee which considered the matter. Some of them were:

- Comrades of the Great War
- Veterans of the Great War
- Liberty League
- Army of the Great War
- Legion of the Great War
- Great War Legion
- The Legion
- The American Comrades of the Great War
- The Great Legion
- The American Legion

The last was tentatively decided upon as the best name although there was considerable discussion on it. This discussion waxed particularly warm between a colonel and a corporal and it came to an end only when some hungry enlisted delegate braved the officer's rising ire to move an adjournment for lunch. The motion carried immediately and, true to the understanding made at the outset in regard to rank, the corporal clicked his heels together, stood at attention and saluted the colonel, when the latter passed him on the sidewalk exactly five minutes after he had been telling the colonel precisely what he thought of him and his opinions—at least as far as the name of the Veteran's Organization was concerned. I might add that this colonel was well under thirty-five years of age and that the corporal was only twenty-one.

And this brings to mind another striking feature of this most unusual gathering, which was the comparative youth of its membership. For instance the two individuals who have taken from the beginning the leading parts in the movement, Bennett Clark, son of Champ Clark and a Lieutenant Colonel of infantry, and Theodore Roosevelt, Jr., son of the ex-president and also a Colonel of infantry. They are respectively twenty-nine and thirty-one years of age, and one of the most brilliant speeches in the caucus was made by a captain of twenty-six.

It must not be understood from this rather dry recital of what took place at the Paris Caucus, this record of minutes and resolutions, that it was an entirely sedate and dignified gathering. On the contrary, Young America was there and quite often the impression which one gathered was that a dozen or so Big Brothers had been turned loose at once. A great many wild speeches were made and all sorts of ticklish questions were brought up. Chairman Clark broke two gavels and three times overturned his table. Everyone there was young. Peace was young. Few knew exactly, like Bishop Brent, just what was wanted. The whole project was new. Dozens of delegates wanted to speak; it was their first chance since April 6, 1917. In fact one man made two very violent speeches on the same subject, one in direct opposition to the other. He realized he was making a heated argument for both sides and finally sat down laughing about it. Who was he? Who was the colonel who got wrought up over the proposed name? Who were the lieutenants, and who were any of these privates, captains, and sergeants?

"I don't know." Nobody knows.

Doubtless they have themselves forgotten what they said. No verbatim records are available now. In fact I am told that no record could have been kept, for many times two or three were speaking at once and the chairman was breaking the third commandment with his gavel. But this much everyone wanted, "A Veteran's Organization." This much everyone swore he would have, one that was neither political nor partisan, one that would perpetuate righteousness, insure "honor, faith, and a sure intent," and despite whatever bickering there might have been, despite whatever differences of opinion arose, when, with a tremendous "Aye," the motion to adjourn was carried, this Paris Caucus had accomplished a body politic and a soul of the type which Bishop Brent so clearly described.

To resume the story of actual accomplishment. The Executive Committee was given general power to represent the units in France, to confer with committees or representatives of the American Caucus as soon as these should be appointed, and, in conjunction with the latter, to issue a call for the holding of county and State conventions and providing a unit of representation and method of selection of delegates to one general convention for the autumn of 1919, preferably November 11th, or Armistice Day.

The Executive Committee met immediately after the adjournment of the caucus and elected Colonel Foreman of the Thirty-third Division, Chairman; Lt. Colonel George A. White, Forty-first Division, Secretary and Major R.C. Patterson, Paris Command, Assistant Secretary. Lt. Col. White, Col. Wood, Major R.C. Patterson, and Lt. L.R. Farrell were elected permanent members at large of the Executive Committee.

Then from this executive committee a committee of fifteen was chosen for the purpose of expediting the work which had been assigned to the larger committee, it being easier to assemble fifteen men than the larger number. The committee of fifteen elected Col. Bennett Clark as its chairman.

At the first meeting of the committee of fifteen a hope was expressed that the caucus in America would take similar action in the appointment of an executive committee, which would in turn delegate its authority to a smaller committee for working purposes. Just exactly how this worked out, is later described.

Chapter Three - Pre-Caucus Days in America

Once home again it didn't take a Solomon to tell Colonel Roosevelt that he had a man's size job on his hands in starting the American Legion on its way in the United States. Dispatches more or less accurate had told the service men on this side something about the Legion activities of the A.E.F. in France. As late as mid-April, however, a great many men in this country knew nothing whatever about the American Legion, while the majority of those who did were not at all sure it was to be *The Veteran's Organization*. What I have said previously about the "spontaneous opinion" of the men in France on the question of a veteran's organization proved to be equally true among service men on this side of the water. Consequently, it wasn't long after the armistice before several veteran's organizations and associations were in the process of formation. As it was a pertinent news topic, the newspapers gave a great deal of prominence in their columns to several of these organizations. They were of various types and characters. One was for enlisted men only. Another was for officers only. There was an organization for officers who had fought in France, Italy, or Russia and there was one or more organizations which had the breadth of vision to see that men of all ranks and all branches of the military and naval establishments must be eligible.

Such was the situation confronting Colonel Roosevelt when he arrived home to help start the American Legion in its own country. The fact of his arrival and his announced intention to aid in the organization of the Legion was duly heralded in the press of the United States.

At first the army and navy men were inclined to say, "Here is another of those mushroom Veteran's Associations bobbing up." In fact I heard one officer make just that remark, but another was quick to correct him by saying, "Its bound to be a straight and honest organization or a Roosevelt wouldn't stand for it." That was the crux of the initial success of the Legion, because just that was true. Every man who wore the uniform had known Theodore Roosevelt, Sr., and although he may not have agreed with him in all of his political opinions still he knew that neither he nor any member of his family would back any organization or proposition that was not morally sterling.

There were those who did not like the American Legion. There were those who were willing to let a past political prejudice deter them from aiding in the most important movement in American life to-day. There were those who stated that Theodore Roosevelt, Jr., was prominent in organizing the American Legion for his own political advancement. The answer to that misapprehension will develop later and will prove one of the most striking incidents in this story.

Colonel Roosevelt has a peculiarly happy faculty of keeping those who work with him cheerful and optimistic. He gathered around him, to launch the movement in America, a set of cheerful, competent optimists, prominent among whom were Colonel Richard Derby, Colonel Franklin D'Olier, who figured in the Paris Caucus, Major Cornelius W. Wickersham, Assistant Chief of Staff of the Twenty-seventh Division, Captain Henry Fairfield Osborne, Lieutenant Colonel Granville Clark, Lieutenant Colonel Leslie Kincaide, Lieutenant Colonel Eric Fisher Wood and Captain H.B. Beers. One of Colonel Roosevelt's first duties as temporary chairman of the Legion over here was to create the nation wide organization. He needed committeemen in every State to work the State organization up, and to start the machinery for the election of delegates to the St. Louis Caucus, for it had been decided that the representation in St. Louis must be by duly elected representatives from congressional districts in so far as that was possible. Each such district was awarded double its congressional representation, in addition to the delegates at large. It was no easy task to pick these committeemen. The decision of the Paris gathering that the organization must be non-partisan and non-political had to be adhered to in its fullest sense. There were soldiers and sailors enough in all the States who would have been willing to have started the organization in their respective localities, but how *not* to get politicians of the lower order, men who would gladly prostitute the Legion, its aims and ambitions to their own selfish advantage—that was the problem which faced the temporary committee in America.

About three weeks before the St. Louis Caucus the following names were chosen from the various States as committeemen:

OFFICERS

Lt. Col. Theodore Roosevelt, Jr., New York, Chairman

Lt. Col. Bennett Clark, Missouri, Vice-Chairman

Lt. Col. Eric Fisher Wood, Pennsylvania, Secretary.

Alabama

Lt. H.M. Badham, Jr.,   Birmingham

Pvt. W.M. Cosby, Jr.,   Birmingham

Sgt. Edwin Robertson, Birmingham

Arizona

Pvt. Ned Bernard,   Tucson

Lt. Col. J.C. Greenway,   Bisbee

Arkansas

Pvt. P.R. Graybill, Democ. Pub. Co. Little Rock

Major J.J. Harrison,   Little Rock

Pvt. Walter J. Wilkins,   Pine Bluff

California

Sgt. L.P. Adams,   San Francisco

Corp. Chas. A. Beck,   San Francisco

Lt. Col. Benjamin H. Dibblee,   San Francisco

Chaplain Joseph D. McQuade, San Francisco

Major Stewart Edward White, Santa Barbara

Colorado

Lt. G.W. Cutting,   Florence

Sgt. C.C. Neil,   Greeley

Major H.A. Saidy,   Colorado Springs

Sgt. Phil. G. Thompson, Denver

Connecticut

Maj. Morgan G. Bulkeley, Hartford

Lt. Col. Jas. L. Howard,   Hartford

District of Columbia

Pvt. L. Clarkson Hines, Washington

Col. E. Lester Jones,   Washington

Delaware

Major Thomas W. Miller, Wilmington

Capt. John P. Nields,   Wilmington

Florida

Brig Gen A.H. Blanding, Bartow

Georgia

Col. Alexander R. Lawton, Jr., Savannah

Capt. Landon Thomas,   Augusta

Idaho

Major C.M. Booth, Pocatello

Pvt. John Green,   Twin Falls

Major Hawley, Jr., Boisé

Pvt. D.H. Holt,   Caldwell

Illinois

Chf. Petty Officer B.J. Goldberg,	Chicago
Maj. Owsley Brown,	Springfield
Rear Admiral Frederick B. Bassett,	Great Lakes
1st Cl. Pvt. Edw. J. Czuj,	Chicago
Maj. Thomas Gowenlock,	Chicago
1st Cl. Pvt. Hy. Hickman Harris,	Champaign
1st Cl. Pvt. Geo. Kendall Hooton,	Danville
Ensign Allen M. Loeb,	Chicago
Capt. Clark Nixon,	East St. Louis
Maj. John Callan O'Laughlin,	Chicago
Capt. Joseph Medill Patterson,	Chicago
1st Cl. Pvt. C.J. Schatz,	Wheaton
Brig. Gen. Robt. E. Wood,	Chicago

Sgt. David S. Wright,   Oak Park

Indiana

Col. Solon J. Carter,   Indianapolis

Ensign Win. L. Hutcheson, Indianapolis

Sgt. R.J. Leeds,   Richmond

iowa

Sgt. Chas. A. Doxsee, Monticello

Major H.H. Polk,   Des Moines

Kansas

Gen. Chas. I. Martin,   Topeka

Gen. Wilder S. Metcalf, Lawrence

Sgt. Fred C. Stanford,   Independence

Sgt. Mahlon S. Weed,   Lawrence

Kentucky

Pvt. Samuel J. Culbertson, Louisville

Lt. W.C. Dabney,   Louisville

Capt. Shelby Harbison,   Lexington

Major James Wheeler,   Paducah

Louisiana

Capt. Allen Cook,   New Orleans

Lt. John M. Parker, Jr., New Orleans

Maine

Lt. Col. Arthur Ashworth, Bangor

Col. Frank W. Hume,   103d Inf.

Capt. A.L. Robinson,   Portland

Pvt. Daniel J. Smart,

Sgt. Wm. H. Whalen,   103d Inf.

Sgt. Freeman Wheaton, 107th Inf.

Maryland

Lt. James A. Gary, Jr.   Baltimore

Sgt. Alexander Randall, Baltimore

Major Redmond Stewart, Baltimore

Brig. Gen. W.S. Thayer, Baltimore

Massachusetts

Brig. Gen. Charles H. Cole, Boston

Sgt. Edw. J. Creed,   101st Inf.

Sgt. Ernest H. Eastman,   104th Inf.

Major J.W. Farley,   Boston

Lt. Col. Louis Frothingham, Boston

Sgt. Geo. Gilbody,   101st Inf.

Sgt. Daniel J. Nolan,

Michigan

Lt. Col. Fredk. M. Alger,   Detroit

Sgt. Rand F. English,   Detroit

1st Sgt. Wm. King,   Detroit

Lt. Commander Truman H. Newberry, Detroit

Minnesota

Pvt. Gordon Clark,   Duluth

Major Paul B. Cook,   St. Paul

Pvt. Wm. D. Mitchell,   St. Paul

Pvt. W. Bissell Thomas, Minneapolis

Mississippi

Lt. John N. Alexander, Jackson

Sgt. Maj. C.J. Craggs,   Greenville

Major Alex. Fitzhugh,   Vicksburg

Corp. Isador A. Frank, Clarksdale

Sgt. Elmer Price,   McComb

Missouri

Brig. Gen. H.C. Clarke,   Jefferson City

Pvt. David R. Francis, Jr., St. Louis

Corp. Sestus J. Wade, Jr., St. Louis

Montana

Col. J.J. McGuiness, Helena

Corp. Chas. S. Pew, Helena

Nebraska

Major P.F. Cosgrove, Lincoln

Pvt. T.T. McGuire,   Omaha

Sgt. R. Scott,   Imperial

Lt. Allan A. Tukey, Omaha

Nevada

Sgt. E.L. Malsbary,   Reno

Lt. Col. Jas. G. Scrugham, Reno
New Hampshire
Sgt. Herve L'Heureaux, Manchester

Major Frank Knox,   Manchester
New Jersey
Col. Hobart Brown,   Newark

Sgt. Allan Eggers,   Summit

1st Lt. Geo. W.C. McCarter, Newark

Corp. Roger Young,   Newark
New Mexico
Capt. Bronson M. Cutting, Santa Fé

Col. Debjemond,   Roswell

Pvt. Canuto Trujillo,   Chimayo
New York
Lt. Col. Robert Bacon,   New York

Lt. Col. Grenville Clark,   New York

Brig. Gen. Chas. I. Debevoise,   Brooklyn

Pvt. Meade C. Dobson,   New York

Col. Wm. J. Donovan,   New York

Lt. Samuel Gompers, Jr.,   New York

Seaman Jos. F. Healey,   New York

Chaplain Francis A. Kelley,   Albany

Lt. Col. J. Leslie Kincaid,   Syracuse

Ensign Jerome H. Larger,   Brooklyn

Ensign W.G. McAdoo, Jr.,   New York

Sgt. Major Howard H. McLellan,   Yonkers

Ensign R.H. Mitchell,   New York

Major General John F. O'Ryan,   New York

Lt. D. Lincoln Reed,   New York

Col. Henry L. Stimson,   New York

Lt. Col. Chas. W. Whittlesey,   New York

Major Cornelius W. Wickersham, New York

Sgt. Clarence E. Williams,   New York
North Carolina
Lt. R.W. Glenn,   Greensboro

Lt. Cyrus D. Hogue, Wilmington

NORTH DAKOTA

Capt. Matthew Murphy, Fargo

Ohio

Sgt. Jas. K. Campbell, Shreve

Lt. Col. Jas. R. Cochran, Columbus

Lt. Col. Ralph D. Cole, Columbus or Findlay

Lt. Col. Isadore H. Duke, Cincinnati

Oklahoma

Sgt. Eugene Atkins, Muskogee

Brig. Gen. Roy Hoffman, Oklahoma City

Oregon

Pvt. Harry Critchlow, Portland

Sgt. Carl B. Fenton, Dallas

Lt. Col. Geo. Kelley, Portland

Col. F.W. Leadbetter, Portland

Lt. Col. Geo. A. White, Portland

Pennsylvania

Major Chas. J. Biddle, Philadelphia

Lt. Joseph F. Frayne, Scranton

Lt. Col. Robt. E. Glendinning, Philadelphia

Lt. Col. John Price Jackson, Harrisburg

Pvt. George Jones, Scranton

Maj. Alexander Laughlin, Jr., Pittsburg

Col. Asher Miner, Wilkes-Barre

Lt. John R. Sproul, Chester

Lt. Bernard J. Voll, Philadelphia

Rhode Island

Major Geo. E. Buxton, Jr., Providence

Col. Everitte St. J. Chaffee, Providence

Sgt. W.C. Kendrick, Pawtucket

South Carolina

Sgt. W.C. Coward, Cheraw

Lt. Chas. C. Pinckney, Charleston

C.T. Trenholm, Charleston

Major W.D. Workman, Greenville

South Dakota

Capt. Lawrence R. Bates, Sioux Falls

Capt. Royal C. Johnson, Aberdeen

Sgt. Ruble Lavery, Vermilion

Sgt. Jos. F. Pfeiffer, Rapid City

Tennessee

Col. James A. Gleason, Knoxville

Sgt. Major Keith J. Harris, Chattanooga

Sgt. John Hays, Memphis

Col. Luke Lea, Nashville

Major T.C. Thompson, Jr. Chattanooga

Pvt. C.W. Tomlinson, Chattanooga

Texas

Capt. Stanley E. Kempner, Galveston

Col. H.D. Lindsley, Dallas

Col. H.B. Moore, Texas City

Utah

Sgt. Maj. H.H. McCartney, Salt Lake City

Gen. R.W. Young, Salt Lake City

Virginia

Pvt. Frank G. Christian, Richmond

Lt. C. Francis Cocke, Roanoke

Col. Stuart McGuire, Richmond

Vermont

Pvt. Donald J. Emery, Newport

Sgt. Eugene V. Finn, St. Albans

Major H. Nelson Jackson, Burlington

Capt. Redfield Proctor, Burlington

Washington

Lt. Col. R.W. Llewellen, Seattle

Major P.P. Marion, Seattle

Brig. Gen. Harvey J. Moss, Seattle

Sgt. John J. Sullivan, N. Seattle

Sgt. Major R.H. Winsor, Tacoma

West Virginia

Capt. Fleming W. Alderson, Charleston

Sgt. Walter S. Moore,　　　　Huntington

Sgt. Thomas Schofield,　　　Wheeling

Lt. Col. Jackson A. Weston,　Charleston

Wisconsin

Edward F. Ackley,　　　Milwaukee

Pvt. David Bloodgood,　Milwaukee

Sgt. Elmer S. Owens,　　Milwaukee

Col. Gilbert E. Seaman,　Milwaukee

Pvt. John P. Szulcek,　　Milwaukee

Wyoming

Major A.S. Beach,　　　Lusk

Sgt. Morris A. Dinneen,　Cheyenne

Pvt. I.H. Larom,　　　　Valley Ranch

United American War Veterans, Warren S. Fischer, Commander-in-Chief

Comrades in Service,　　　　　Bishop Brent, President,

National Legion of America,　Major Elihu Church,

American Army Association,　Lt. Haywood Hillyer, General Secretary.

　Just about this time it became most necessary to properly present the Legion to those men who had remained at home and who had gotten out of the Service, and to those who were incoming from France and rapidly being demobilized, as it was upon them that the success of the Legion depended. Furthermore, their opinions were the soil upon which the various State organizations had to work, and at that particular time it was vital that the Legion should be widely known and thoroughly understood; that its aims and ambitions should not be misconstrued either willfully or unintentionally, nor its precepts perverted. To this end the temporary Chairman proceeded to publicize it in the most thorough fashion. One-page bulletins briefly outlining the Legion's aims and ambitions were distributed in every center where soldiers and seamen gathered. Such places as Y.M.C.A. and K. of C. huts and War Camp Community recreation centers were thoroughly informed, and bulletins also were sent to every ship in the navy with the request that they be placed on the ship's bulletin board.

　Literature about the Legion was placed on transports when they left empty for France so that the men might read it in their leisure hours returning home. In order to make sure that every soldier and sailor would have the opportunity to know about the Legion this literature was again placed on the transports as they arrived in New York harbor. Various demobilization camps throughout the country were widely placarded and in each instance the names of the Temporary State Secretaries were given, and service men were invited to write to the Secretaries in their particular States. Camp publications, newspapers, and periodicals published for service men throughout the country were bountifully supplied with Legion information and scores of them carried special stories in regard to it. Bulletins and pamphlets were distributed in hospitals, placed on bulletin boards, and given to the patients. Every mayor of a town or city with a population above nine hundred got a letter containing literature about the Legion with a request that it be given publicity in the local press and then turned over to the Chairman of the Welcome Home Committee. Certain national magazines devoted a great deal of space to special articles explaining the Legion.

Three or four times a week the Foreign Press Bureau of the United States Government sent stories about the Legion and its activities by wireless to the ships on sea and to the men of the A.E.F. in connection with its "Home News Service." In addition to the foregoing, articles appeared almost daily in the press throughout the entire country, and by the time the convention was ready to meet those who ran and cared to read were fully informed that the American Legion was an organization for veterans of the army, navy, and marine corp; that it was non-partisan and non-political; that it stood for law and order, decent living, decent thinking, and true Americanism.

The wide publicity given to the Legion and its aims brought into the Temporary Committee many amusing letters. Scores of them complained of the published statement that it was non-partisan and non-political. "Damn it all, we want it to be political and partisan," one angry Westerner wrote. Another correspondent insisted that in view of the fact that sons of Theodore Roosevelt, and Speaker Champ Clark were interested, the Legion must be bi-partisan and bi-political. But most of the letters were of a highly commendatory character, expressing the deepest and widest possible interest. I recall that one of them came from Junction City, Kansas, another from Old Town, Maine; one from Delray, Texas, and others from Wolf Creek, Montana, Orlando, Florida, and Ray's Crossing, Indiana, while a postal card making frantic inquiries was dated Nome, Alaska, and arrived a week after the caucus at St. Louis. I have mentioned these towns and localities because they indicate how widespread and deep is the interest in the Legion. No matter where a man came from to go into the army, the Legion will go to him in his home now. Its members will range from fishermen on the Florida Keys to the mail carriers on the Tanana in Alaska, from the mill hands of New England to the cotton planters of the Mississippi delta. All who wore the uniform may enroll just so long as the word *Americanism* was inscribed in their hearts between April 6, 1917, and November 11, 1918.

Chapter Four - The Advance Committee

When the St. Louisian puffed its way into the big smoke-begrimed station in Missouri's largest city I looked about me for Bill, who was going to meet me at the station. We had not met since our prep. school and college days when Bill had been a thin, wizened little fellow, so hollow-chested that he had to be sent to Colorado for almost two years for his health. He came back to school looking better but before his diploma was handed to him announcing to the world that he was a full-fledged Bachelor of Arts, he had fallen apparently permanently into the rut of ill-health. In fact I wondered, when we all sang *Auld Lang Syne* in the fraternity house at the close of college, if I'd ever see Bill again.

From time to time I had heard from him in the years that followed, and one day in the summer of 1917 he wrote me that he was on the way to France.

While I gazed up and down the smoke-laden platform, I got a slap on the shoulder that sent me spinning, and there was the once emaciated Bill, who seemed to have grown three inches and to have put on seventy-five pounds.

As we walked toward the taxicab stand I began to realize that instead of an old friend, a stranger was beside me. True enough, he had the same name and the same colored eyes, and his hair hadn't changed. But the rather dreamy eye had cleared, the pale face of old was tanned, and Bill's chest—the one he had gone to Colorado for—was bulging out as he carried my two heavy suit cases like a pouter pigeon's at a poultry show.

What had happened to Bill? The little, quiet, timid youth of the past was now a big, burly, strong-bodied, clear-minded man. As we entered the taxi he was telling me that he "intended to raise hell if they didn't take some action against this blank Bolshevism, and furthermore that this new Legion was going to be the most tremendous organization that the U.S.A. had ever seen." If he had told me that Swinburne's *Faustine* was written in iambic hexameter it would have sounded more like old times. But here was a new man, strong and virile, intensely interested in the future of his nation.

What had happened to Bill? Eighteen months in the army was the answer.

The advanced delegation began to arrive in St. Louis, the afternoon of May 5th. The Statler and Jefferson Hotels were packed because there were two other conventions in progress. But our delegates needed no badge to be distinguished from the others; there was a difference between them and the other conventionites. There was the same difference between the two as between the old Bill and the new Bill. They too had had eighteen months in the army, and a coat of tan on each one's face, his ruddy frame, and general atmosphere of a healthy mind and a healthy body were unmistakable emblems.

This advanced delegation, two from each State, had been requested to come beforehand to meet on the morning of Tuesday, May 6th, so as to formulate a working order of business on which the caucus might proceed as soon as it assembled. There was another reason for this meeting also. The temporary committee wanted to avoid any appearance of having "framed up the caucus." By this it is meant that the committee wanted to be able to say to the caucus that its working procedure had been determined by a thoroughly representative body, a democratic, advanced delegation composed of men from every State in the Union. There were those critics of the Legion, who, had the temporary committee formulated the caucus procedure, would have been only too glad to have attempted to make trouble by saying it was a controlled and made-to-order caucus—controlled and made-to-order by the men who had taken the lead in it. In fact, during the early morning of the first day the advanced committee met one delegation arrived with blood in its eyes determined to wage a fight against universal military training. One of the stories circulated at the time was to the effect that the entire Legion was nothing but a blind whereby a mysterious "Military Clique" was to gain supreme power over the Legion's policies. It took but a very short while to convince the would-be obstreperous delegation that the caucus was not the convention and was empowered solely to organize a veterans' association and not to adopt policies.

The temporary committee in America determined at the very beginning that no policies would be adopted at the caucus, that the Legion at this time should follow in the footsteps of its comrades abroad in stating that neither the men here nor the men there could, as different units, adopt broad policies until a convention could be held truly representing all men who had fought in the Great War.

Colonel Roosevelt called the advanced committee to order a little after two o'clock in the afternoon, in a small and very noisy parlor in the Hotel Statler. The gavel which he used was made from wood from the rudder of Admiral Peary's North Pole steamship *The Roosevelt*, which had been presented to him by Colonel E. Lester Jones of Washington, D.C.

"The idea underlying the formation of the American Legion is the feeling among the great mass of the men who served in the forces of this country during the war, that the impulse of patriotism which prompted their efforts and sacrifices should be so preserved that it might become a strong force in the future for true Americanism and better citizenship," Colonel Roosevelt said. He spoke very slowly and measured his words carefully but emphasized them in a tone of deepest conviction. "We will be facing troublous times in the coming years," he continued "and to my mind no greater safeguard could be devised than those soldiers, sailors, and marines formed in their own association, in such manner that they could make themselves felt for law and order, decent living and thinking, and truer 'nationalism.'"

In this opening sentence, Colonel Roosevelt foreshadowed the spirit of the entire caucus. These service men wanted an organization not for their own special benefit, not that they might obtain pensions or offices, but that they might become a power for truer Americanism and better citizenship!

Colonel Wood, the secretary, explained in greater detail the purpose of the proposed Legion. He broached the subject of the reemployment for soldiers, a legal department for the handling of insurance claims, allotments, etc., and sketched the fundamental principles of the organization as follows:

First, its non-partisanship.

Second, that this society should be equally for those whose duty called them overseas and for those who were held by circumstances on this side.

Third, that it is fundamentally a civilian organization, one in which all ranks, be they private or general, admiral or seaman, should have an equal share and participation.

Then the advance committeemen began themselves to talk. Each one, no matter on what subject and regardless of the side he took upon it, was permitted to air his feelings to the full satisfaction of himself at least. Like the Paris Caucus, the discussion grew heated at times and every now and then the chair was forced to remind overly fervid orators that this was an advanced meeting of the caucus and not the convention. There were those present who wanted to obligate the caucus to go on record for or against universal military training, woman suffrage, prohibition, permanent headquarters, and to elect permanent officers, and each of these had to be shown that it would be unfair to the men still in the A.E.F. to take such preëminently vital steps without consulting them. Then there were those present who wanted to exclude members of the regular army and navy from the Legion; that is, to limit eligibility in the organization to those who could show discharge papers from either the army, navy, or marine corps. This measure was voted down and it was given as the sense of the advanced committee meeting that those who served in the Great War would have perfect liberty to join regardless of whether their service continued in the military establishment after the armistice or after peace was formally declared.

The advanced committee outlined the order of business upon which the caucus could proceed, named the various committees to be organized, and discussed the resolutions which were deemed wise and expedient topics for discussion.

On Wednesday afternoon, delegates from every district in the country began to arrive, almost one thousand new Bills, husky of frame, some still in uniform with the red discharge chevron on their left sleeves; others who had manifestly tried to get the new Bill into the old Bill's 1916 suit of clothes, and still others in new bib and tucker, looking exceedingly comfortable after almost two years in putties, heavy shoes, and tight blouses.

Every man came with one deep-rooted determination and that was to see that no one "put anything over" which might make an organization so embryonically useful take a fatal or selfish step. Each came, perhaps imbued to a certain extent with his own particular ideas on how everything should be conducted; but the radicalism, sectionalism, and partisanship which would have marked a gathering of these same men three years before was not present. The men who had thought that nothing good could come except from south of the Mason and Dixon line had fought side by side with woodsmen from Maine. The man who had thought the East effete had done duty on a destroyer with a boy from Harlem. Everybody realized full well that sectionalism must be abandoned whenever it clashed with nationalism; and abandoned it was, with right good will.

The meeting of the advance committeemen justified itself as a very wise and judicious action on the part of the temporary committee. Any suspicion of a particular delegation that anything was "framed" was quickly allayed after a conference with its advance committeemen. If a man from Pennsylvania suspected that anything was on foot not to the liking of the Keystone State he had only to ask his advance committeeman, Colonel D'Olier, about it. Incidentally the personnel of the advance committee was not so numerous that everybody couldn't know what everybody else was doing. As a matter of fact, everybody did know what everybody else was doing. One of the most peculiar facts of this most interesting caucus was that when it came to "*pussy footing*" pussy seemed to foot it on piano keys so far as secrecy was concerned and in such a fashion that usually the *Star Spangled Banner* was played. I know that the night and the morning before the caucus met that there were many and various powwows and conferences, a great many of which I attended, but there wasn't a one that I knew of or ever heard about, the full details of which could not have been printed in bold-faced type on the front page of every St. Louis newspaper and have reflected credit on the powwowers as well as on the American Legion.

Chapter Five - The St. Louis Caucus, May 8, 9, and 10

All during the morning of May 8th that delegation was constantly getting together with this delegation; this leader conferring with that one; was this question going to come up, and what would be done if that question was tabled? Everybody interested, everybody excited, everybody waiting to see the other fellow's hand at the show-down, which was scheduled for the Shubert-Jefferson Theater at half-past two o'clock in the afternoon. Of course, everybody had found out the previous evening that every card in the pack was red, white, and blue, and that, from the very beginning of the game, an attempt had been made to keep the knaves out. As a matter of fact, they'd never been in, but the new Bills who made up the delegations to this caucus were going to look everybody over mighty carefully before any serious playing was done.

Suppressed excitement doesn't describe at all the half-hour preceding the opening of the caucus, because the excitement was not suppressed in the least. Eager, shining, tanned faces, eyes alert, heads erect, straight-bodied and straight-talking men one by one took seats which were assigned to them by delegations.

A flashlight photograph of the gathering was made, but this caucus was not one that could be pictured by the camera at all accurately. The outstanding feature of this great get together was the spirit of the men, and that no camera could catch.

Three large wooden tiers of seats, the kind the circus has under canvas, were built in a sort of semicircular fashion around the large stage. The New York delegation occupied one of these tiers; the Ohioans another, while the third was built for distinguished guests. If any distinguished guests came they were entirely put out of the limelight by the audience, for this was one show which was enacted before the footlights rather than behind them, and, with one or two exceptions the star performing took place where the spectators usually sit. In fact, the only spectators that I saw were the newspaper men, seated at tables within the corral formed by the tiers. All of them had been in the army or navy or had seen the big show abroad as war correspondents.

When Theodore Roosevelt, as temporary chairman jammed that gaveled bit of the rudder of the North Pole ship down hard on the table and called the meeting to order he got what he had never received while in the army: that is, direct disobedience. He commanded order, and there was utter disorder. It was rank insubordination, distinctly requiring court-martial of everyone present, from a military point of view—but the American Legion isn't military! And so the delegates howled joyously. Roosevelt, demanding order at this time, had just about as much chance of getting it as the Kaiser has of making Prince Joachim King of the Bronx. Somebody started a cheer, and the crowd didn't stop yelling for two minutes and a half.

"Young Teddy," as they called him, was manifestly surprised at the ovation and tried repeatedly to get the crowd quiet. He wanted to be pleasant and yet he wanted order and so between knocks with his gavel he smiled. And a very engaging smile it was, too.

"Gentlemen," he pleaded. "Gentlemen, a little order." Finally there was comparative quiet. "Now let's proceed to the business of the meeting. The floor is open for nominations for permanent chairman of this caucus."

Sergeant Jack Sullivan of the State of Washington got the floor. Sergeant Jack is a husky northwesterner who did his bit in the intelligence section in Seattle and has seen a lot of the Bolsheviki out there.

"In behalf of the State of Washington and representing the men of the rank and file of the Pacific Northwest, it gives me pleasure at this time to place for your consideration the name of a sterling patriot," he shouted. "The man I am going to place in nomination proved himself to be a one hundred per cent. true blooded American when his country's honor was assailed. He was among the first who placed himself in the front-line trenches, he was wounded twice, he was ready and willing to make the supreme sacrifice in order that this world might be made safe for democracy. I deem it an honor and a privilege, and the Pacific Northwest deems it an honor and a privilege to place in nomination the worthy son of a worthy sire—Theodore Roosevelt."

The crowd seemed to know all along who Jack meant and it held its enthusiasm in tether as best it could. But when Sullivan got to the word Theodore, the Roosevelt was drowned out in the mightiest cheer that is possible for eight or nine hundred throats to utter. The second to the motion, made by Colonel Luke Lea of Tennessee, wasn't heard at all. This time it took Colonel Roosevelt more than two minutes to get order.

"Gentlemen, I want to speak on that now," he shouted and during a lull in the cheering managed to make himself heard. "I wish to say that I want to withdraw my name from nomination—"

But the "gang wouldn't hear to it." Somebody raised the old cry:

"We want Teddy!" "We want Teddy!" "We want Teddy!" they chanted in unison. Bedlam broke loose at that. Men stood on their seats and waved their hats and handkerchiefs; some took their collars and neckties off; some wept, some cursed for sheer joy and others—I believe that when Gabriel blows his horn and all the dead arise that some of the men who attended that caucus will try to make a speech! These speeches were going on four and five at a time during the entire hullabaloo. It didn't seem to matter in the least to the speakers that they weren't being heard. They couldn't hear themselves. They added a little to the noise and that satisfied the crowd and seemed to satisfy them.

"Please, please let me talk," pleaded Colonel Roosevelt. He finally got his plea over by means of the sign language.

"I want to withdraw my name for a number of reasons," he continued. "The first is that I want the country at large to get the correct impression of this meeting here. We are gathered together for a very high purpose. I want every American through the length and breadth of this land to realize that there isn't a man in this convention who is seeking anything for himself personally; that all of us are working simply for the good of the entire country. I believe, furthermore, that what we want here is someone who has been connected with the movement only since it started on this side of the water, someone who originates from the convention."

The din started again.

"No, no, gentlemen," shouted the Colonel. "I want to withdraw. It is my earnest wish. It is my absolute determination."

But the caucus seemed equally determined. "We want Teddy!" "We're going to have Teddy!" "You got this thing going, you ought to run it." Colonel Roosevelt paced up and down the stage, trying his best to silence them. Then, during the din, one by one some of his oldest friends went to him and begged him to accede to the crowd's wish. "Take it Ted," they urged. "Take it." That underslung jaw of the young Colonel's became rigid.

"I won't do it. I can't do it," he answered.

Then someone managed to make a motion that the nomination of Colonel Roosevelt be made unanimous. It was seconded and made extremely *unanimous.*

Theodore Roosevelt, Jr.

"Then, gentlemen, I accept and I resign," Colonel Roosevelt said. "I want quiet for a moment here on this situation. This is something that I have thought about and have given my most earnest consideration. I am positive I am right on it. We must not have creep into this situation, in which we all believe from the bottom of our hearts, the slightest suspicion in the country at large. I don't think there is any suspicion among us that anyone is trying to use it for his personal advancement. But it is absolutely essential that this spirit be proven. I am going to stick by this from the beginning down to the very end because, in my opinion, we have got to create to-day the impression all over the country on which this organization will carry on and serve a great purpose for years to come."

Again there were outbursts of applause for the Colonel. "We want Teddy!" "We want Teddy!" the crowd cried again and again. Men ran to the stage from the orchestra seats and even from the second balcony.

"Take it, Colonel. You ought to take it," they urged.

What the Colonel answered couldn't be heard but the jaw was working and the head was shaking vigorously.

A couple of newspaper men dashed up to him.

"You oughtn't to take it, Colonel," one of them whispered. "If you don't, it will give the lie to those who are saying the Legion is being conducted for your special political benefit."

"I haven't the slightest intention of taking it," he answered back.

He didn't take it and he nailed the lie that the Legion was started to further his own selfish ends.

On motion of Colonel E. Lester Jones of the District of Columbia the nominations were reopened again.

Sergeant Haines of Maine put up the name of Colonel Henry D. Lindsley, a banker of Dallas, Texas, and a prominent Southern Democrat, for permanent chairman. Think of it! A man from Maine nominating a Southern Democrat! One of the Ohio delegation seconded the nomination. Think of that too! Colonel Claud Birkhead of San Antonio, Texas, leader of the Texas delegation "thirded" the nomination. He told Colonel Lindsley's record. The Colonel had been Mayor of his home city, and during the war had served his country so well in France that he had been awarded the Distinguished Service Medal. He and Major Willard Straight, now dead, had started the War Risk Insurance Bureau abroad and, at the time of the caucus, Colonel Lindsley was the head of the Bureau under the Treasury Department in Washington.

Minutes of a meeting usually are dry but here I am going to quote directly from them because they tell the story in the most vivid way. Fancy between the lines, please, dozens of cheers, a couple of rebel yells, a great deal of talking and shouting for "T.R.!" "T.R.!" and a Babelous babble that ebbed or flowed according to the strength Colonel Roosevelt used in wielding his gavel.

Colonel Jones (of Washington, D.C.): "Mr. Chairman, I personally feel, and I think I voice the unanimous sentiment of this organization, that your withdrawal is a mistake. We are not only sincere, but we are telling you what is in the bottom of our hearts. We are weighing also the sincerity which you have expressed, and in deference to your wishes, which I know have not arisen spontaneously but which you have talked about for some time, regarding the chairmanship of this committee, I think we should not embarrass you further. I have one in mind who I feel is going to be a man who will do credit to this organization—"

Mr. Abbott (of Ohio): "Gentlemen of the caucus, I think we are wasting time around here. I can't see why we can't have for the permanent chairman of this convention the man who will be elected in November."

The Chairman: "Gentlemen, can't you see how it is? I can't possibly change my convictions. I can't go back on what I have told you without everybody, who doesn't understand the situation here, feeling that I have just come out here to make a grandstand play. I am right. I am absolutely sincere and right."

A motion was made that Colonel Theodore Roosevelt temporarily yield the chair to Colonel Bennett Clark.

Colonel Bennett Clark: "It is very evident what the desire of this convention is. I know that Colonel Lindsley of Texas was only put in nomination in response to the express wishes and repeated determination of Colonel Roosevelt. I think that that explanation should be made in justice to Colonel Lindsley. I think that Colonel Roosevelt should take this chairmanship or if he doesn't want to take it he should be made to take it. (Applause.) The chair will recognize a motion to that effect."

Captain Boyce (of New York shouting to a yelling audience): "What is the use of our acting like a lot of kids? Just one minute; only one man can talk at a time and get anywhere. Colonel Roosevelt will not take it."

Colonel Bennett Clark: "The chair will recognize nobody until the convention is in order. It has been moved and seconded that Colonel Roosevelt be elected chairman of this convention by acclamation."

Cries of approval from the audience and a request for the question.

Colonel Bennett Clark: "On that the chair will take the responsibility of ordering a roll call. (Applause.) The Secretary will call the roll."

Secretary Wood: "The motion is that Colonel Roosevelt be nominated by acclamation. The chairman has directed me to call the roll by States. Alabama-"

A call for a point of order.

Delegate: "After nominations have been made and closed a roll call cannot be taken."

Colonel Clark: "The chair was fully aware that he was proceeding outside of parliamentary law because it was the unanimous wish of the convention."

Mr. Sullivan: "I move that a roll call be made on the original nominations."

Colonel Clark: "Colonel Roosevelt has expressed to me his absolute desire that that not be done. He refuses to enter into a contest with Colonel Lindsley in any way."

Colonel Jones (Washington, D.C.): "Mr. Chairman, the nominations were reopened."

Colonel Clark: "The chair is informed that while he was on the way up here a motion was carried to reopen nominations after the resignation of Colonel Roosevelt. Now nominations are again in order."

Major Samuel D. Royce (Indiana): "On behalf of the State of Indiana, I nominate Colonel Theodore Roosevelt."

The motion was seconded.

Colonel Clark: "The gentleman from the District of Columbia has the floor. Others please be quiet."

Here I must inject my story into the minutes again. Colonel Roosevelt saw the convention was "getting away to a Roosevelt finish" again, to use a racing term, and he sent a hurry call to the Arizona delegation for Colonel Jack Greenway.

Jack Greenway followed the elder Roosevelt up San Juan hill. He wears underneath his civilian coat to-day, but right over his heart, a Distinguished Service Cross won at Cantigny.

"Jack, for Heaven's sake, tell them I won't take it," Colonel Roosevelt plead.

It was just at this moment that Colonel Clark, the acting chairman, was saying: "The gentleman from the District of Columbia has the floor. Others please be quiet...."

Colonel Jack waving one arm at the chairman and another at the audience strode to the center of the stage.

The minutes read:

Colonel Jack Greenway: "Will you give me the floor? I won't keep you five minutes.

"My name is Greenway but that doesn't mean anything to you. Gentlemen, Colonel Roosevelt has said that he is not going to take the nomination of the caucus and you can take it from me that he is not going to do it. Now wait a minute. Whoa! Quit yelling! I know this Roosevelt outfit and when they say something they mean it. I followed his daddy through Cuba and I know. I saw this boy in the first division at Cantigny and on the Toul Front and I know that he means he is not going to take the chairmanship of this temporary caucus. There is a big misunderstanding about what you are trying to do. I have just talked to Colonel Roosevelt and he says that he will not be a candidate for the temporary caucus, but if, after all the boys come home at the convention in November, it is still the desire of that body as a whole, he will give the matter reconsideration." (Applause.)

Colonel Roosevelt resumes the chairmanship.

The Chairman: "Mr. Lindsley, the gentleman of Texas is in nomination for chairman. I mean absolutely what I say. I can't do it. I won't serve if elected. What you have done will always be a great memory to my family. (Applause.) I mean that, gentlemen! I mean that! Now is there anybody else you want to put in nomination? I absolutely mean that for the good of the cause; you have got to do what I say on that.

"Gentlemen, I believe the nominations were reopened."

Now I must again put the minutes by for a moment, for Bill has come to the stage and what he says doesn't get into the minutes, although I wish his remarks were there:

"That was pretty fine in him," Bill said, pointing to Colonel Roosevelt. I nodded only, for somehow this whole thing had got to me pretty strong and I felt like crying for some unaccountable reason.

"And then he gives his family the credit for all this yelling," Bill was saying. "We like his family all right, but say, this wasn't to compliment his family, not by a darn sight. Why, you know that young Colonel's got a h—— of a fine record himself—"

But somebody within an inch of my ear was letting out a warwhoop for Jack Sullivan who had just been nominated for permanent chairman and I didn't hear the last of Bill's remark.

Sergeant Sullivan got up and tried to withdraw in favor of Colonel Lindsley, and Colonel Lindsley did the same thing and each was refused the opportunity. Colonel Lindsley then took the floor. "Comrades," he said, "I want you to know that I came here for one man for the chairman of this caucus, and that man was Theodore Roosevelt. He has refused it absolutely. I appreciate the support that has been given to my name. If honored with the chairmanship I shall be glad to serve, but it is important that we get to business immediately. I am certain that Mr. Sullivan will make an excellent presiding officer. If I had the right, I should be glad to withdraw my name in his favor. But the point is, gentlemen, let's get to business. This is the greatest meeting that has ever gathered in the United States, and it is not so material who is chairman of the meeting as it is to proceed to business."

While the roll is being called let's glance around the theater again. Most of the men in uniform are enlisted men. It is difficult to tell at a glance just what rank or rating the majority of those present held in the army or navy because in civilian clothing the officer and the man are indistinguishable. I mean to say that our army was different from most other military establishments. Being primarily a citizen affair it was really representative. It was the desire of the temporary committee that sixty per cent. of the delegates should be enlisted men and when the call for the caucus was issued that was set forth most plainly. No one seems to have taken the trouble to check the thing up at the caucus. Anyone desiring to do so can find the information in this volume. I was interested at the opening of the caucus to know just what the percentage was, but after it got into swing it didn't make any difference. No one cared. There was talk (among officers) of making an enlisted man permanent chairman. The only persons that I heard objecting to such a procedure were the enlisted men themselves.

"We've forgotten all that stuff about rank. If the officers insist on an enlisted man they'll make a mistake. We want the best man and because we're in the majority in the organization we don't want to discriminate against the officer. Taken as a whole, he was a mighty fine sort."

This from Sergeant Laverne Collier of the Idaho delegation when I asked him what he thought of the enlisted man idea. While we were talking about it the vote was being cast on Lindsley and Sullivan. As if to reecho Collier's sentiments, Sullivan got up and demanded that Lindsley's election should be made unanimous, and so it was.

Colonel Roosevelt promptly put Sullivan's name in nomination for vice-chairman. Mr. Abbott of Ohio seconded it and further moved that the sergeant's election be made unanimous. Sergeant Jack Sullivan was elected by acclamation. Then Colonel Wood was chosen secretary, the rules of the

House of Representatives were decided upon to govern the procedure, and debate was limited to five minutes.

Insistence on that point was unnecessary. Our new American back from the wars has been too accustomed to action to like words that aren't concise and aimed right at the heart of the point. There was a good deal of noise and talk at this particular juncture and someone moved the appointment of a sergeant at arms. Captain A.L. Boyce of Boyce's Tigers (those young men who drilled so persistently in Central Park in New York preparing for the war) was picked. While this guardian of the peace was being appointed at least five gentlemen from as many delegations started to speak at once, perhaps against the five-minute debate rule, and in the confusion a delegate, whom Checkers might have described as carrying a load he should have made three trips with, took the platform and began something that sounded about as intelligible as Cicero's oration against Catiline in the original.

"Do I understand, Mr. Chairman, that a sergeant at arms has been appointed?" shouted Mr. J.L. Walsh of the Pennsylvania delegation.

"That's right," answered the chairman.

"Then let's have him get busy," rejoined Mr. Walsh. "We didn't come down here for a vaudeville show or to be entertained by some boob, because we've got boobs back home."

After this remark, the minutes read "Laughter and applause" but that doesn't half describe it.

Captain Boyce "got busy" and if the minutes could record the result of his actions they would probably read "Order restored—almost. Quieter, for a time."

Colonel Lindsley made a splendid presiding officer. None could have done better, but as the stenographer who took the minutes remarked (and she was convention-worn because she had attended so many): "This is the funnest meeting I ever wrote up." Right. It was the funniest meeting—funny being used in the sense of unusual as the stenographer meant it—that anyone ever saw. In fact it was unique; absolutely the only one of its kind. Because the delegates were unique. There never was anything like them in all the history of the country. They had gone into training camps like Bill, very tired, anæmic, with a shop and office pallor; and they came out of the war like Bill,—new, virile, interested, placing a value on themselves which would have been unthinkable prior to April 6, 1917.

But they placed a greater value on this organization which was so near the heart of all of them. No better proof of it can be shown than the incident which has just been described, viz., the refusal of Theodore Roosevelt to be the permanent chairman. Although I do not pretend to be able to explain the processes of thought and reasoning which led Colonel Roosevelt to take the action he did, still I do know this much! There are very few young men who would have been so deaf to the plaudits of the multitude, to the advice of old friends and to the still small voice of personal ambition as he was in refusing. I maintain that this refusal was by no means altogether prompted by anything of an hereditary nature but, rather, by the experiences and environment which had been Colonel Roosevelt's during the war. It took more than an under-slung jaw and a rugged Rooseveltian determination to refuse this great honor. It took *discipline*, and Colonel Roosevelt knew how to inflict that upon himself just as he did upon his troops whenever it was wise and necessary.

In much smaller, but no less important matters, did I see other men practice discipline upon themselves. I saw men forego the discussion of subjects in which they believed with all their hearts and with all their minds solely for the purpose of doing nothing that would tend to disrupt the Caucus or give the impression throughout the United States that the men who had stuck together so closely in times of daring and danger could not still stick and face, as a band of brothers in the American Legion, any perils or pitfalls which peace might hold for this country. Therefore, it seems to me that Colonel Roosevelt's action was more than a manifestation of his own sterling determination to do nothing which might hurt the Legion. It was archtypical.

Major Hamilton Fish of New York called attention to the fact that the navy was unrepresented in the offices of the caucus and moved that a second vice-chairman should be appointed from that branch of the service. A delegate from Missouri seconded the motion and amended it to read that a third vice-chairman should be appointed from the marine corps.

During the election of these officers enthusiasm reached a high pitch and in no more striking manner did the new American reveal his new character.

"Gentlemen," said one dignified delegate (I don't know who let him in, because just from the way he said "gentlemen" we all knew that once in his life he had practiced oratory before the bureau mirror), "I want to place in nomination the name of a man who is true blue—"

"Name him," shouted the crowd.

"He is not only true blue but he is thoroughly everything he ought to be in addition—" continued the orator, coldly trying to squelch the crowd.

"Name him." "Shut up." "Aw, sit down." "Who wants to listen to such 'bull' as that?"

Each of those sentences was roared by a different man.

"This gentleman is one of whom I am sure you will be proud—" persisted the orator, but at this direct violation of its edict the crowd began to scream its maledictions and Captain Boyce could not have stopped them with all his Tigers if the gentleman orator hadn't taken his seat in a most dignified manner, never to rise again—doubtless as a rebuke for the gang, but one which was thoroughly appreciated.

Thus the way of orators in the caucus!

The navy men who were nominated consisted of Goerke of New York; Goldberg, Illinois; Chenoweth, Alabama; Almon, Montana; Humphrey, New Mexico; McGrath, New Jersey; and Evans of Kentucky. The secretary took the vote by delegations. When Goerke got a vote the New York crowd yelled itself hoarse; New Mexico did the same for Humphrey; Alabama cheered like mad for Chenoweth and it wasn't long before everybody picked out his candidate and yelled furiously every time he got a vote. The New Mexico delegation occupied a proscenium box but Humphrey wasn't prominent enough there to suit his delegation. Before anyone thoroughly realized what was happening, Seaman Humphrey appeared on the stage, borne on the shoulders of two colonels! Two men who had eagles on their shoulders, U.S. on their collars, and gold chevrons on their left sleeves carried on their shoulders a "gob," a sailorman, a deck-swabbing bluejacket, as he called himself.

It was the beginning of a cavalcade of noise that fairly made ear drums ache, and, incidentally, proved a signal for the backers of other candidates. Goerke soon was lifted aloft by a half dozen New Yorkers; Chenoweth was exhibited to the general view from the section of the orchestra occupied by his delegation, while Illinois paraded up and down the aisles with Goldberg. Colonel Lindsley hammered the speaker's table almost to pieces in an attempt to get order and then gave it up for a few minutes as a bad job. Captain Boyce succeeded in getting a semblance of it, when everybody got tired of carrying the candidates and of shouting. Then the secretary again started taking the vote by delegations. No one of the candidates received a majority of the votes which was necessary under the procedure adopted at the beginning of the caucus. Then began the withdrawals. This State withdrew its vote from Goerke and cast it for Humphrey; Chenoweth withdrew from the race and his vote went to Goerke, et cetera. A similar situation resulted on the second count and finally Goerke withdrew in favor of Humphrey. When Evans took the same action, Humphrey (first name Fred), described as the "rough-riding sailor from New Mexico," was elected.

Humphrey's speech of acceptance delighted the hearts of those who had forced the would-be orator to sit down at the beginning of the nominations.

"Mr. Chairman, gobs, soldiers, and marines," Humphrey said: "I am most glad and gracious to accept this honorary position and I will do everything that a deck-swabbing sailorman can do to fill it."

The first day's session closed with the appointment by the various States of representatives on the following committees: Executive Committee; Credentials; Temporary Name of Organization; Organization; Resolutions; Constitution and By-Laws and Declaration of Principles; Next Meeting Place and Time; Publication; Emblem; Permanent Headquarters, and Finance.

The personnel of these committees will be found elsewhere.

Thursday evening and Friday morning were devoted largely to committee meetings and different sections of the country came together to discuss matters of particular interest to special localities. For instance, the Western delegations discussed the question of Bolshevism, because the symptoms of this mad disease had been more apparent in that section of the country than in any other. The question of color was practically decided in a meeting of the Executive Committee and was ratified later by various delegations representing the Southern States. Everybody was pleased. An attempt was made by the leaders of each delegation to keep such questions as might be "*loaded with dynamite*" off the actual floor of the caucus so that those lacking in discretion might not have the opportunity to throw the caucus into an uproar.

In fact it was this spirit—the desire on everybody's part to give in to a certain extent on any mooted question for the sake of general harmony that was a marked feature of the gathering. In the committee meetings were found delegates with radically different opinions on almost every question. It was not an uncommon thing, however, to see a delegate very heatedly advocate a certain side of an issue; listen to the opposing side, rise, and with equal heat and fervency advocate the opposite point of view.

This spirit is highly significant. It will be one of the Legion's greatest powers. It was and is due to the fact that these new Americans are not cursed with fixed ideas. They have seen too much, lived through too much in their comparatively short lives to be narrow-minded. Over in the A.E.F. the former hod-carrier often turned out to be too good as a construction manager for any officer to despise his opinions. One noticeable characteristic of the American Legion delegate was the respect which he had for the other man's views and his willingness to admit outright that he was wrong in a thing or to go at least halfway with the opponent of his particular ideas. This was the saving grace of the caucus and this will be the saving grace of the Legion for the spirit which was manifested there is the spirit which will prevail at Minneapolis, and for always, because the American sailor and soldier will not change.

It was interesting to see these modern American soldiers side by side with the veterans of the Civil War. The Grand Army of the Republic Post, the local Bivouac of the United Confederate Veterans, and the Spanish War Veterans gave a joint reception for the delegates at the Missouri Athletic Club which included a smoker and a vaudeville entertainment furnished by the War Camp Community Service.

Chapter Six - The Legion and the Bolsheviki

The second session of the caucus began at half past two o'clock Friday afternoon. Like its predecessor it started with a bang. Nominations were made for the third vice-chairman who was to be selected from the marine corps. The first nomination was a wounded man, at the time in the Walter Reed Hospital at Washington and who had won the Distinguished Service Cross at Château-Thierry. Then came the name of Sergeant Woolley of Utah, quickly followed by the name of P.C. Calhoun of Connecticut, put up by Mr. Black of Louisiana; the name of Major Leonard of the District of Columbia also was put in nomination and then the slate was closed.

True to the spirit of the previous meeting the caucus was soon in an uproar of applause for each of the four candidates, three of whom were marched to the stage. Calhoun was elected, with the result that his ardent brother delegates from Connecticut treated him like a football hero by placing him on their shoulders and performing a snake dance. Marines are no more garrulous than sailor men, for Calhoun's speech of acceptance was just about as long as Humphrey's. While Calhoun was being bombed by flashlight cameras Mr. Smoot of Utah moved that a vote of thanks should be tendered to Colonel Roosevelt and other Legion members who had been active in the preliminary work which insured the success of the caucus and this was seconded by Major Wickersham of New York. One of the most rousing ayes of the entire caucus carried the motion.

Cries of "speech" brought Colonel Roosevelt before the footlights. His remarks were just about as long as Humphrey's and Calhoun's. To be specific he said: "Gentlemen, it is going to be a short speech because I think we have got a lot of business to do. Thank you."

Just about this time the committee reports began to come in, the first of which, that of the Credential Committee, brought the question of Bolshevism to the floor of the caucus. The report read as follows:

"We recommend that all delegates to the American Legion selected and now functioning from the various States, districts, and territories, be seated and accredited with full vote, and that all organizations organized and having delegates here be allowed one vote with the exception of the Soldiers and Sailors Council, which delegation the Credential Committee recommends shall be excluded from the caucus."

S.H. Curtin, the representative of the Soldiers and Sailors Council of Seattle, pending the action of the Credential Committee, had been accorded a vote at the previous session on all questions that came up before it. The fact that Colonel Wood, the Secretary, took this action was in line with the general spirit of fair play, which was the keynote of the caucus. The Credential Committee's report elicited shouts of approval. Chairman Lindsley after bringing the house to order again said:

"I understand that the delegate from the Soldiers and Sailors Council is here and asks to be heard. Gentlemen, the members of the Committee, I assume, had full knowledge of facts which warranted that report, but there are men here who have not that knowledge. Shall we hear him?"

This statement aroused mixed emotions but Mr. Curtin came to the platform. Word having spread through the theater that he represented the "real Bolshevik outfit" in Seattle, a great many of the delegates began to hoot, jeer, and make cat calls.

"Give me a square deal, give me a hearing," Curtin shouted.

"Give the man a hearing," echoed Colonel Roosevelt, who sat with the New York delegation. "Yes, give him a hearing." shouted the majority of the delegates and when the chair had procured order, Curtin made his plea.

"I wish to say, by way of introduction, that though I come from the State of Washington, I am not a member of the Washington Delegation," he said, "I say that out of deference to the members from that State for the reason that I wish to prejudice nobody here against the Washington Delegation. I am not an I.W.W. I never have been and I never intend to be I never have shown any Bolshevik tendency and I defy any man present to prove to the contrary. If you've got proof that Sherman H. Curtin ever was an I.W.W. or made a Bolshevik statement, say so?" He paused here but none answered him to the contrary

"It is true that the organization which I represent has had in the past some I.W.W.'s, and it is true that there are some I.W.W.'s in it now," he continued; "but I am in that organization for the purpose of throwing those I.W.W.'s out. I got in there for the purpose of kicking them out and I want your help."

Here he was interrupted by applause.

"At the present time, we (when I say we, I mean the particular conservative element which I represent in that organization) have control of the Board and practically all except one office of the organization. We are doing everything in our power to make that a one hundred per cent. American organization, and one of the things that I came down here for was to see that the Legion had in its constitution as a preamble that we pledge ourselves to the principles of democracy as set forth in the constitution of the United States of America.

"I, personally, was the man who rewrote the constitution of the Soldiers and Sailors Council. It was written wrong when I got in there so I changed it. I want you men to stand behind me and help me make this fight. My organization did not give me permission to come here and join this, just as I presume some of your organizations did not give you permission, for the reason that they did not know what this was going to be; but I can see from the spirit that this organization has, that so far, it is on the right path and I am with it and I want you with me.

"I am already only and wholly for the purpose of doing what good we can for the elimination of I. W.W.'s and Bolsheviki. If you are against that, I am with you and if you are with me, I am with you.

George Pratt of Louisiana rose.

"With your permission," he said to the chairman, "I would like to ask the gentleman one question." "Sir," turning to Curtin, "is it or is it not true that you re-wrote the constitution now in effect for your organization, and is it not true that it is so worded that American Army and Naval officers or former army and navy and marine officers of the United States are not eligible? Is that true?"

"I will answer that question and I will answer it in a fair way," Mr. Curtin replied.

"Say yes or no. Is it true?" Mr. Pratt demanded.

"Yes," shouted the crowd. "Say yes or no. Is it true?"

Then pandemonium broke loose in the meeting. The cat calls and boos were renewed. "Put him out!" "Put him out!" "Shut him up!" the crowd demanded. And here I want to pause a moment to say that the enlisted men present gave a mighty concrete sign of the approval of their officers by this denunciation of the constitution of Curtin's outfit.

"I am not here for the purpose of being persecuted," Mr. Curtin shouted. "I am not asking no or yes to anything. But I will say to the gentleman who questioned me that while it is true in letter it is not true in spirit."

At this juncture Mr. Simon, of the Washington delegation, said that in all fairness to Sergeant Curtin he wanted to say that during the recent demonstration of Bolshevism in Seattle, Curtin commanded a machine gun company on the side of right and law and order.

"I do not speak for his organization," Simon said, "but I speak for a clique in it, headed by Sergeant Curtin, who went into that organization to clean it up, to make it a fair and square one hundred per cent. American organization." The applause of Simon's remarks had scarcely died down when General Moss succeeded in gaining the floor.

"I want to say to the members of this delegation," he said, "that I led the fight against the soldiers' and sailors' organization before the Credential Committee, and I want to say to you gentlemen that we didn't lead a fight personally against this man, but against his organization.' We know the outfit in our country and we do not want that organization in unless the Americans in it come in as individuals. I want to say that we are to be organized here on a basis of one hundred per cent, true Americanism.

"I asked Curtin in the presence of the committee if he represented a minority or a majority in his outfit and he admitted that he represented the minority."

"But we can lick a majority," Curtin shouted back. "I want Captain McDonald who had charge of the Intelligence Department at Camp Lewis to say a word on this subject. He knows the history of my organization and I would like to have him give it to you." But if Curtin counted on McDonald to help him he reckoned without his host.

Captain McDonald rose and speaking with great deliberation said:

"I have been an American soldier for thirty years. I was a regular telegraph officer at the time of the Bolshevik trouble. I established stations at Seattle and Camp Lewis and this man represents the real element that we are all working against. Personally he is all right but he is backing that organization because he wants to represent it. If he desires to be admitted into the Legion let him get loose from that outfit and come in by himself."

Captain McDonald's statement was greeted with enthusiasm.

"Are you ready for the question?" demanded the chairman.

The caucus certainly was.

"Those favoring the adoption of the credentials report vote aye," he cried.

That aye could almost have been heard in Seattle itself.

That aye answered the question of what the American soldier thinks of Bolshevism or anything tainted with it. That aye answered the lying statement that our troops abroad had been inoculated with the germ of the world's greatest mental madness.

That aye marked the distinction between a grouch caused by a cootie-lined bunk and a desire to place a bomb under the Capitol at Washington.

I have intimated that the chief aim of each delegate was to see that no one "put anything over" at this caucus. I think that the only other determination which might rival that in intensity was most apparent at the mention of anything that pertained to or bordered on Bolshevism. This incident of ousting Curtin's organization was not the only manifestation of it by any means, although it was perhaps the most striking on the floor of the caucus. But, outside the caucus, in the hotel lobbies, and in the various committee rooms, whenever the subject came up these soldier and sailor men, in almost every instance, got mad—damn mad.

"The trouble with these people who talk Bolshevism is that they don't know anything about our country," I heard one of them say.

Another quickly interrupted him with, "The big thing the Legion's got to teach is Americanism and let those crack-brained fools know just what this country stands for." While still another injected, "The average 'long-beard' has been so crazed by persecution in Russia that he would mistake Peacock Alley in the Waldorf-Astoria in New York for a Siberian coal mine."

This last remark brought forth a laugh, and though it was whimsically made it illuminated the matter under discussion very well, I thought. In fact, the whole conversation made clear to me one of the fundamental missions the Legion must perform.

The seeds of Americanism which Legion members sow to-day will be reaped, not only to-day but in the generations of to-morrow. The Soldiers and Sailors Council, Seattle, was thrown out and its representative knew why. But, if Jack Sullivan and his red, white, and blue colleagues in the State of Washington preach in the future what they did at this caucus, the children of those northwestern Bolsheviki will not only salute the Stars and Stripes, but will know *why* they do so. They will know what their fathers don't—that the constitution means Americanism and that Americanism means "life, liberty, and pursuit of happiness."

In most conventions the reports of committees are invariably adopted. There are many reasons for this, the particular one being the theory that when a set of men are placed on a task they will study the situation in all its angles, in all its ramifications, in all its different phases and that its report should therefore be adopted because of this expert thought and study on the matters under consideration. I say that most conventions do this. Once as a newspaper man, I attended an undertakers' convention. It always did so. And at another time I attended a manufacturers' gathering where this procedure was invariably followed out. But how about at St. Louis? Not on your life! The delegates of the American Legion were neither like undertakers nor manufacturers nor like any-other business men that I ever saw during ten years on a Metropolitan newspaper. The new American doesn't do business that way.

Witness the report of the Committee on Name. This report read: "We, your Committee on Name, unanimously make the following recommendation—that the name of this organization be the American Legion of World War Veterans." The chairman had scarcely finished asking: "What is your pleasure gentlemen" when Major Wickersham got the floor and moved an amendment that the name be "The American Legion." This was seconded by Mr. Cochrane of Ohio and then came the argument about it.

Mr. Shank of Ohio, thought that the American Legion did not convey a sufficient meaning to the average civilians. "The American Legion might be an organization of street cleaners, it doesn't signify soldiers. It isn't comprehensive enough," he said. Mr. Larry of Florida countered with, "Go ahead and call it American Legion, we will soon show them what it means."

Mr. Walsh of Pennsylvania, suggested that the A.E.F. knew what it was doing when they called it the American Legion. "Let us honor them and respect them by calling it the American Legion," he urged. Colonel E. Lester Jones, of Washington, stated the name had been considered by the committee most carefully and—

But why go into all the arguments. The motion to call it the American Legion was carried amid cheering and as such the name will go down into the history of things well done for America.

Chapter Seven - The Legion Won't Meet at Chicago

We have arrived at what is the most significant event of this session of the caucus, if not of the entire gathering. The caucus has already shown its spirit in ousting the Soldiers and Sailors Council because, in its opinion, it could not measure up to one hundred per cent. Americanism, and now we shall see what the same simon-pure brand of red, white, and blueism is demanded of the second largest city in the United States.

It came about in the most dry, matter-of-fact way. Let the minutes of the meeting form the introduction for it.

The Chairman: "Next is the report of the Committee on the Next Meeting Place and Time."

Secretary Wood (reading): "From the Committee on Next Meeting Place and Time, to the Chairman of the American Legion; action of the Committee.

"Meeting called to order at 10:30 A.M. this day at the Shubert Jefferson Theater.

"Charles S. Caldwell, of New Mexico, unanimously elected chairman.

"Frank M. Ladd, Jr., of Alabama, Secretary.

"The majority of the States being represented as per attached list voted unanimously for Chicago as next meeting place. Date being set as November 10, 11, and 12, 1919.

"Respectfully submitted,

"CHARLES S. CALDWELL, *Chairman,*

"FRANK M. LADD, JR., *Secretary.*"

Mr. Sexton (of Illinois): "When you consider your place for your next convention tell Chicago what you want, and in response to that Chicago will answer you. 'We will give you whatever you want.'"

Then the excitement started. Mr. Dietrick of Pennsylvania moved to amend the report of the committee. "By striking out the word Chicago and substituting therefore the city from the State which furnished more soldiers than another state—the city of Pittsburgh."

This elicited great applause—especially from the Pennsylvania delegation. Mr. Stems of Louisiana got the floor—

"I want to tell you what took place in that committee," he said. "The committee selected a place to the best interest of this organization and not to the best interest of any one specific locality, and the question was argued in a very quiet, organized, gentlemanly manner. A number of the delegates put up towns that did not get enough support to get the meeting, so they withdrew their names. It was all to the interest of the organization so it was unanimously adopted by that committee, without any dissenting vote, that Chicago be unanimously adopted as the place for the next convention for the best of all interests concerned. I am from New Orleans, Louisiana, which is a convention city and I will not offer my city to you as a convention city at this time because I do not think it is to the best interest of your country."

Bennett C. Clark
Who presided at the Paris Caucus

When Mr. Stem took his seat at least a dozen delegates clamored for recognition from the chair. Colonel J.F.J. Herbert succeeded in getting it. It was he who then fired the gun which, if not heard around the world at least made Chicago's ear drums rattle.

"Mr. Chairman," he began—

Colonel Lindsley rapped for order.

A man near me whispered, "There's Herbert of Massachusetts. I think Boston is too far east for this convention, at least for the first one."

Colonel Lindsley got order, and you could have heard a pin drop, while the following statement was made by the Massachusetts leader:

"As the spokesman for my delegation on this question of next meeting place I want to say that if no other body and if no other party of this caucus wants or believes it is its duty to rebuke any city or the representative of any city for Un-Americanism during the time when the soldiers of that city were offering their lives in defense of the world, then Massachusetts stands ready to offer that rebuke. Massachusetts will not agree willingly to having a convention of soldiers and sailors in the Great War, go to a city that has as its first citizen, by vote, one who can not measure up in any small part when the test is one hundred per cent. Americanism."

When Colonel Herbert reached this point one delegate with a big voice from a big State (Texas) let out a loud yell of approval. This was the signal for blast after blast of vocal vociferousness which fairly raised the roof. Men stood on their seats, and cheered. "You're dead right" and "Get a new mayor, Chicago," while others began to point at placards advertising Chicago which had been placed on the walls of the theater by members of the Illinois delegation. Colonel Herbert stood for fully five minutes before order was sufficiently restored for him to proceed.

"The hall has been placarded with invitations, reading, 'The American Legion, Chicago wants you in November,'" he said. "I believe that this convention, this convention of soldiers and sailors should say, 'Chicago, you cannot have American soldiers in Chicago when there is a possibility that the chief representative of that city may not believe it is his duty to come before the Convention and welcome it.' If these placards read, 'American Legion, Chicago *soldiers* want you in November,' our answer might be different. The answer of Massachusetts would be different but when your placard reads, 'Chicago wants you in November' the answer of Massachusetts is, 'Chicago cannot have us in November'—or any other time until Chicago has an American for Mayor in an American city.

"The literature circulated through the caucus reads, 'Chicago pledges itself to go any other city one better on anything this convention requires.' This convention first requires that Chicago shall reach a standard different from the standard of being the most despised city in America, and when it has reached that standard, it is then in a position to say whether it can go one better. It has not yet reached par. Until Chicago reaches par, Massachusetts votes no!"

A large poster reading "Chicago bids you Welcome," had been placed over the seats directly in the center of the stage; Captain Osborne pulled it down. This was the signal for similar action all over the house. Chicago banners, dropped from the boxes, were hurled to the floor. Other banners which had been on the theater walls just out of reach were torn down by men who climbed on the shoulders of their fellow delegates in order to reach them. Only during the ovation given Colonel Roosevelt, did the cheering reach such intensity.

These men were cheering for Americanism. They wanted one hundred per cent. Americanism, untainted and unvarnished by a hyphen or an "ism," especially when the word pacific precedes the latter. Everyone felt sorry for the Illinois delegation, for it was realized that Colonel Herbert's

Eric Fisher Wood

Secretary

remarks were intended solely to reflect upon the person he specially mentioned and not upon the thousands of soldiers and sailors who went from Illinois and Chicago and did more than their part in writing glorious history.

Just how this was impressed upon the men from Illinois let the minutes show. The chairman recognized "the gentleman from Chicago."

Mr. Cummings (of Chicago): "Gentlemen, I don't believe there is a single delegate to this caucus who would be so unfair as to impugn the patriotism of 650,000 men who rallied to the colors of this country by saying: 'Because Chicago had a mayor of which they are all ashamed that they are not patriotic.' Had the men who were serving the colors in France been in Chicago, they would have had no apology to offer for their mayor. (Applause.) He was elected in a three-cornered fight where he did not receive a majority vote in Chicago, but had the opposition to him been solidified he would have been

snowed under, for Chicago is patriotic. I consider that an insult has been handed to every man in Illinois who rallied to the colors.

"The Tank Corps of which I am a member, and an enlisted man originally, gave from Chicago 11,250 enlisted men, volunteers in the most hazardous branch of the service. They gave 11,250 men as against 11,000 which the rest of the country contributed. If that doesn't bespeak patriotism for Chicago, I don't know how you are going to gauge it. I am saying that in the invitation which was extended to you we are speaking for the boys of khaki and blue who rallied to the colors from Illinois, and who are here to-day, extending the invitation to you notwithstanding the fact that we are cursed by a mayor who is not our choice. We would throw him out if we had the chance, but we are extending the invitation to you on behalf of 750,000 men from Illinois and we do not feel that you are going to impugn their patriotism, that you are going to insult them by saying they are members of an unpatriotic community."

Mr. Hawkins (of Oklahoma): "The great State of Illinois stands unchallenged in the patriotism of its soldiers throughout the world. I am only sorry that you didn't leave enough patriots at home to elect a patriotic mayor of that great city. You are in the embarrassing position of having a man who has repudiated the things we went out to die for. Either you have got to repudiate us or repudiate him."

"We'll repudiate him next time when the boys get home," shouted several of the Illinois crowd.

Then other speakers tried to make it plain that the Legion's attack was solely against the municipal head of Chicago, but some of the men of Illinois let the incident rankle. How it came out (and it was ended happily) will develop. Meantime the attention of the caucus was diverted from the Chicago incident by the manifestation of that desire which is in every true American's heart, namely to be a booster for his own home town. In less time than it takes to tell it, Los Angeles, Minneapolis, Atlantic City, St. Louis, Pittsburgh, Indianapolis, Kansas City, and Chicago were being voted upon. While the delegates were voting, a small body of soldiers and sailors were gathered together in a wing of the theater, seriously discussing the incident which was developed by Colonel Herbert's speech. They desired that it should be made more plain to everyone just what Colonel Herbert meant and that the millions of patriotic simon-pure Americans who live in Illinois should not take undue umbrage of the incident. Therefore while the vote on the convention city was being counted, Colonel Luke Lea was recognized by the chairman and asked unanimous consent to present for consideration the following resolution:

"Resolved, That the action of the caucus of the American Legion in refusing to accept the invitation to hold its next convention in Chicago is no reflection upon the splendid patriotism of the men and women of that great city, who have loyally proved their Americanism by supporting our Army and Navy and all war activities.

"Be It Further Resolved, That this caucus records its admiration of the valor and heroism of the thousands and thousands of Chicago's sons whose pure patriotism has been proven on the battlefields of France."

"I would like to say something in support of the motion," Colonel Lea said. "It is very proper for me to offer it for I had the privilege of serving for three months with the great Thirty-third Division of Illinois and I know what wonderful soldiers they are."

The resolution was adopted by unanimous vote.

No booster ever had a better time than had those who attended the St. Louis Caucus. Local pride assumed its highest pitch during the vote, and at length Minneapolis won it. The date was set for November 10-11-12th.

Just before adjournment Colonel Herbert arose to a question of personal privilege.

"I would like, if possible," he said, "to have the attention for a few minutes of every man that is in this theater. Intentionally or otherwise, and I think it was otherwise, the soldiers of Illinois have felt that I was not just to them in the remarks that I made bearing on the report of the Committee on the Next Meeting Place. I meant to say, and I believe now that I did say, that if those banners that were hung in this theater had read, 'American Legion, Chicago's *soldiers* invite you next November.' Massachusetts' answer would have been 'Yes.' I believe I said that. The men of Illinois believe I did not say it. The men of Illinois believe that when I sat down after making the few remarks I did, that I had a sardonic smile on my lips and they say that I have insulted them to the heart and I say to them: 'If there is anything that I can say, anything that I can do, as soldier to soldier to remove from your mind, or from the minds of any man who may have been in this theater, any belief that there was any feeling except of highest admiration, the highest respect, and the deepest affection on the part of the soldiers of Massachusetts for the soldiers of Illinois, then I want to correct that impression, because I want you, the soldiers of Illinois, to know that we recognize in Massachusetts that no better soldiers wore the khaki, no better sailors wore the blue, than the men of Illinois. My remarks were, as I stated, for the purpose of saying Massachusetts would, if no other State would, take such action to rebuke the city of Chicago; would say to Chicago that if it would have the right to invite Americans to meet in that city, first Americanize the City Hall. That was my chief purpose of rising to my feet. If Chicago's soldiers, if Illinois' soldiers still think that I have not made reparation for what they believe was the intention of my remarks, then I say to them that no higher respect, no deeper affection exists for them than in the hearts of the men of Massachusetts."

Colonel Herbert's assault upon Chicago's mayor in itself is only half significant. It is only wholly so when its reception is considered. Colonel Herbert will have none of Chicago until it has purged itself of its municipal leader. He remembered, perhaps, the assertion that it is "the sixth largest German city in the world." He might have said as much in a newspaper interview as he said on the floor of the caucus had he been asked about the Illinois city as a meeting place for soldiers, and, perhaps, the editor would have given to it a half column of space; in the larger dailies, less. But when men of the army, navy, and marine corps, from every battlefield in France, from every State in the union, voice their approval so thunderously; when they stand on their seats and cheer; when they so positively overrule the recommendation of committeemen who have studiously considered the matter, presumably from all angles, it means much. No wonder Metropolitan dailies devoted columns to it.

Those of you who have become low-spirited over your own particular view of the future; those of you who have talked about "the good old days"; or, the Spirit of '76, take heart. Take counsel of the Spirit of '19, based on the deeds of '17 and '18, on the mistakes of '14, '15, and '16. '19 is all right!

Read the constitution of the American Legion to-night just before you go to bed. Think of this second day's session when the Bolsheviki-tainted organization was thrown out, when the second largest city in America was told to "clean house" and redecorate in red, white, and blue. Then go to bed and know that all's right with the United States.

A large number of the delegates attended, on the second evening, a dance and supper at Sunset Inn given in honor of the Legion by the ladies of St. Louis. For most though, there was work in plenty to do. Some of the committees hadn't yet reported and there was an all important meeting of the executive committee in the Statler Hotel.

I said *all important* by design. The caucus had taken up a great deal of time with the proceedings already recounted and it was the purpose of the executive committee on adjournment-eve to get down to brass tacks. It certainly did that. It was agreed to recommend to the caucus that the Legion should attempt to help get returning soldiers and sailors positions and that a legal department should be established which would aid men to get back pay and allotments, while still another department would look after their insurance and instruct them how to change it to policies of a permanent character. Needless to say these conclusions were not arrived at without a great deal of helpful discussion.

Then too this executive meeting was all important because it let several persons who claimed to be dissatisfied, air their grievances, thereby clearing the atmosphere of considerable cloudiness. For the most part these malcontents didn't seem at first to distinguish between the caucus and the November convention. They didn't seem to catch at first hand the spirit of the A.E.F. caucus which positively refused to take action on large questions of policy until the Home Army could be consulted. The principal leaders of the caucus in St. Louis determined upon the same course, as has been previously explained, and rightly so. One thing one element wanted to do was to elect permanent officers. "How could you do that when more than a million men entitled to a vote are still in France?" they were asked. They couldn't answer. Another element wanted to go on record against universal military training while still others were for endorsing it. Someone else wanted this city to be chosen as permanent headquarters while another wanted some other town selected. There was some grumbling to the effect that the caucus had been too "rowdy." Then, too, everybody was more or less tired out and a darker view of things was natural.

The silver lining was there, however, as it always is. This time it took the rotund form of a preacher from Alabama. Inzer was his name and his folks and Colonel Roosevelt's away back five or six generations ago in Georgia had been the same people, so let's introduce him as Colonel Roosevelt's cousin. Chaplain Inzer had been ready to embark at Newport News with his regiment when the Bolsheviki menace grew quite serious in the Pacific northwest and he was ordered to proceed to Seattle and was there during all the stirring times which culminated in making Ole Hanson famous.

It might truthfully be said that the "silver lining" quite properly had a silver tongue. When he had spoken just about a hundred words even the grouches were holding onto their chairs if they weren't using their hands for purposes of applause. And many a man, who thought he'd talked his voice silent dug deep down in his vocal chords and brought forth something that could easily be labeled a cheer! This preacher told everybody who might have the slightest idea of making trouble just where to get off. But I am not going to try to remember his speech and perhaps improperly quote the chaplain. The speech was so good that they made him do it again at the very opening of the caucus the next morning, so I'm going to lead off with it in my story of the proceedings of the last day, just as the stenographers recorded it.

Chapter Eight - The Silver Lining

Soon after the caucus opened on Saturday morning, May 10, the minutes read as follows:

The Chairman: "Gentlemen, before we have the report of the Resolutions Committee, I want to say to those who were not of the Executive Committee and in its meeting last night, that there seemed to me to be there a more splendid crystallization of the real purpose of this caucus and a foresight into what it is going to mean, not only to these four millions of men but to the people of the United States for the next half century, than I have ever heard, and at the request of a number of those who were there at that meeting, I am going to ask one of them to interpret to you in just a few minutes, as well as he can, and he did it wonderfully well last night, the spirit that we believed in that meeting is your spirit here to-day and the spirit that is going out from this caucus as a slogan to all American citizens and through them to the world, indicating the purposes for which we fought, and more than that, the purposes for which American manhood stands and for which it will fight again, if necessary, the heritage we will hand down to our children, and I will ask this gentleman to present that thought to you."

Chaplain W. Inzer (of Alabama): "Gentlemen, I appreciate this opportunity more than I have words to say, and if you will only be as sympathetic with me for these minutes as that Executive Committee was last night, I will do my best to interpret the spirit and the mind of this convention as I see it and as I saw it last night. I never had a more sympathetic audience, it seemed to me, or a more psychological moment in which to speak than that was last night and I appreciate the spirit of the brethren who asked me to come out and make this talk this morning and I am going to try my best to interpret it as I saw it last night.

"There has been an undercurrent all through this Convention. Somebody has been afraid that we are going to do something or pop some lid off that will bust the thing and I have been, as I said last night, sometimes scared almost to death. I think I could personally say that I wanted to make about seventy-four speeches in the two days that I have been here. I didn't do it but I was waiting and praying for the psychological hour to arrive and I believe that that hour came last night when this Executive Committee really got together and got something concrete before them, and I think that the whole Convention comes together this morning ready to take up matters of importance and leave off matters that should not be taken up, and to solidify this body in a great spirit of Americanism that shall last for fifty years as the greatest organization that the world has ever known." (Applause.) "Now the keyword that I want to say in the beginning is, at all costs we want to save this organization. We do not want anything to arise to-day that will in any way mar the spirit of this great assembly and the work that it is going to do in the future. While you were deliberating here these past two days some of you thought only of this hour and this moment, but, gentlemen, I had an eye cast into the future and I was dreaming dreams and seeing visions of the years that are to come and the wonderful work, the wonderful influence, and the mighty power that this organization is going to have and exert upon this nation and upon the whole world, and I want you to think of it in these terms. This convention is a baby and we must not choke this baby. You can't give a young baby a gallon of castor oil the first week. It only requires castoria, that is all the first week. It can stand with a little mother's milk, and I want you to feel that way about it to-day." (Laughter and Applause.)

"Our first duty is beyond the shadow of a doubt to get this infant on its legs, and once we get it on its legs, it will be like the mighty Niagara Falls, there isn't anything in the world can dam it up. It will be a power that shall be known, and with influence all over America and for good all over the world. Let's be quiet and let's be sensible to-day until we get this infant on his legs. He's just a recruit, a raw recruit, and he has to be trained and we are going to do that now.

"Gentlemen, I want to say just here, if you can only think about this Legion—the chairman spoke of it last night to me—as the jewel of the ages. I believe that is the best interpretation I know. I cannot say anything greater than this: I believe God raised up America for this great hour; I can say that the strong young man of the time is to be the American Legion in this country and in the world.

"What the great seers of the past ages have dreamed and what they have planned and longed for, the opportunity that they sought, have suddenly been placed and in our hands. Are we going to be great men and big men? Will we arise to the dignity and be worthy of the occasion?

"I believe that we will. Oh, men, if I might make it plain to you that it seems to me I stand on the very rim of creation and I am speaking there to an angel who has never yet been able to see light. I said: 'Angel, what are you doing here?' and he said: 'I was placed here when God created this world'; and he said: 'God sent me to look down upon this world and report to him at one special time, and that one time only,' and I said: 'What was to be the nature of that report?' He said: 'God made man in His own image and God Himself is a being of knowledge, love, truth, democracy, and peace,' and He said to that angel, 'Don't you ever leave that world until you see dawn, until you see that man has come up to the place where he will begin to measure up to what I expected of him,' and that angel said to me, 'I have sat here through all the ages and I have seen times when I thought that the sunlight of God's great knowledge and love and truth was going to come over the hills and then some being like the Kaiser or Alexander or Napoleon or some one that was of a Bolsheviki type would rise up and retard it and the sun could never rise,' but he said: 'Thank God on April 6, 1917, I reported back to God when America entered this war that I had seen the dawn.' (Applause.)

"As little as you dream, maybe when you came here and as little as you thought about it in the commitment of time, I believe to-day that we stand on the dawn of the realization of the republic of man which is nothing short of the Kingdom of God on earth when men shall be men." (Applause.)

"So the first thing we are to do to-day is to get a great spirit, men, a great spirit that we can carry back. All the other questions will be ironed out in due time. Everything will be straightened out when we realize that five million men are going to be organized with the same spirit of love and loyalty and devotion and sacrifice and democracy that characterized their lives on the battlefield. They will never rest until they make this whole world bloom in love, democracy, peace and prosperity and equality and brotherhood for all mankind. That is what we are going to do and that is what this assembly means to-day. It is the world's great opportunity and your privilege to share with it.

"Now, then, I want to say that the soldier spirit is going to be my spirit and I believe it is going to be your spirit. When Wilson and the other men called us to the war, I was glad and ready immediately to offer my life because of the great principle. I said to those men last night in that Executive Committee and I mean it to-day, I'd gladly lay down my life to-day if laying down my life meant that this Legion should live and fulfill my dreams of its service to the country for these next fifty years. (Applause.) So do you think I want anything to come up here that would disrupt this body? Never! Do you think I want to make a fiery speech about something because it is my personal conviction? No, I have a hundred personal convictions that I would like to see operating in the United States and this convention, but it isn't the time and I am not going to bring them up here. I don't want to say anything that will keep all of us from pulling together like a military army for the great things that this convention in the future is going to stand for. So my final word is this: That this day, we get right down to business and that we omit everything that we can omit pertaining to the permanent policy of this organization that we cannot all immediately agree upon.

"If there is going to be anything discussed here to-day that everybody in this convention won't immediately agree upon and would hinder us from sending out to the nation word that we stand together and that we are going to pull together, that we caught a mighty vision and that we have gained the great spirit, then, brethren, let's carry that thing over until November when all the boys come home and then we will discuss it there. There are many things to-day that we can discuss that are important and fundamental and that are urgently needed in our nation this hour. Let's take those things up and get down to business on it to-day. Every Executive Member from each State pledged the chairman last night that he was going to act as a sergeant-at-arms in his delegation and hold the convention in order to-day. We are going to do the right thing and we won't be 'busted' by anything or by anybody, and when anything comes up that isn't the right thing for us to do to make a great impression on America, and the world, we will say hold that thing over until the baby is strong enough to do it right.

"I beg you to do those things. Somebody said: 'What are the things we can do to-day?' We mentioned them last night.

"Jack Sullivan has problems out there that we must meet this very day. One of those is this Bolsheviki business. We are going to pass resolutions this very day, I believe, asking the United States in Congress to pass a bill for immediate action of deporting every one of those Bolsheviki or I.W.W.'s out yonder." (Prolonged Applause.)

"Gentlemen, I know what I am talking about. You don't know how badly I do hate some of those guys. If it hadn't been for them I would have gotten on the boat in Newport News in 1918 for France, but because of those rotten scamps I was sent to Seattle, Washington, and had to stay there for seven months guarding the interest of the shipbuilding in the Western States.

"I was naturalization officer for our regiment and that division out there and I have had those scamps stand up and say: 'Yes, I have been here fourteen years and have lived on the fat of the land, but we don't want to fight,' and they would deny citizenship papers or cancel their first papers.

"Now that the war is over, they are in lucrative positions and our boys haven't got jobs; we've got to say, send those scamps to hell." (Prolonged Applause.)

"We can all see this very moment that there is no division on that question. We stand together. Somebody said: 'Why, we have been here two days and haven't done anything but elect officers and decide on a place to meet. But let me tell you, Buddy, while we have been doing those things, we have let the world know where we stand for Americanism. (Applause.) And we couldn't have done a bigger thing than create the impression we did relative to Mayor Thompson of Chicago and the I.W.W.'s of Seattle. (Applause.) We can do that. We are agreed on that. The baby can do that without any trouble at all and we are not going to choke him when we start that kind of thing.

"The other question that we might decide here to-day is what we are going to do about jobs for our returned soldiers. In my city we have already said: 'Look here, man, you'd better post every job that is open and post it in the place where we get employment for returned soldiers. And they have gotten down to that. We want to talk about that to-day and get down to business— the business of getting jobs for our men, and then we want to care for those who come back without money. We want to help them get their allotment and get their $60 bonus, and we want to care for the wounded.

"But these other things—excuse me, I can't help but say brethren, because I am a preacher, but you are my brethren, I thank God you are and I love you like I love the brethren of my church. There is some fellow here who might want to spring something because he knows it would be a lot of fun. Oh, brethren, let's not have any fun with the baby to-day. (Laughter and Applause.) We have all we can do to-day. We have all we can do if we do those things that we are all united upon and agreed upon. Those things which may have what they call a nigger in the woodpile, when they come up, let's say that is something we are going to talk about later when the boys get home in November, when everybody is settled down and we have thought it through and talked about it in our State organizations and we will come up with solidified ideas and the great spirit will have gripped us and we will know where we stand and will know our power and strength.

"Brethren, I say let's cut out every last bit of hoodlumism to-day. It is the zero hour. Let's stand together. If we don't carry anything else home, let's go home and say we are for America, that we caught the spirit and the vision and you can't stop us with anything in the world. I thank you." (Audience rises and applauds.)

That speech has been given in full not only for the reasons which have been stated before but because it is archtypical of the deep-seated, serious, and high-minded soul of the New American, born of the war.

"Mr. Chairman, it seems that Illinois caught the spirit of the speaker who has just seated himself, in advance."

Before the applause over Inzer's speech had ended and before we realized it, Mr. Cummings of Illinois had the floor. He said that the Illinois delegation had been ungracious in accepting Colonel Herbert's explanation of his remarks the previous day.

"We wish to withdraw that implication," Mr. Cummings said. "We wish to state to you as a solid Illinois delegation that we give full faith and credit to the high, patriotic motive which prompted this gentleman in making the speech to you which he did and in bringing before this organization the question which he did. We feel on cooler deliberation and upon giving the matter the thought which its importance demanded, that he is helping us and that he has placed the American Legion in a position to help us to move in a body politic, to overcome certain things in the State of Illinois and blot out pro-Germanism.

Gaspar Bacon

Treasurer

Cornelius W. Wickersham

Henry G. Mathewson
California

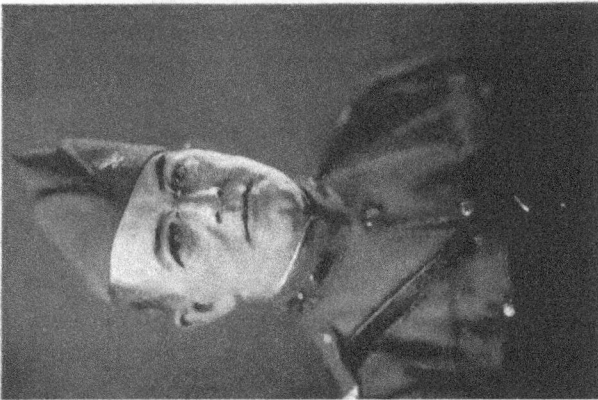

John F. J. Herbert
Massachusetts

Three State Chairmen

"I say that the American Legion is bigger than any man; it is bigger than any State; it is bigger than any combination of States; it is the unified action of the millions of men who were willing to sacrifice their lives, their fortunes, their all on the altar of this country for the cause of democracy, to make the world safe for democracy, and they are going to help us make Illinois come to the front and clean its skirts of the stigma which is attached. We know that you are going to help us in it, and with the support of the American Legion, nothing will stop us from cleaning our skirts, from washing our dirty linen at home. When the next convention of the American Legion is held, as soon as we have had an opportunity or the boys in khaki and blue have had an opportunity to give an honest expression of views on the question of Burgomaster Thompson, we will come through with clean skirts, we will stand before you without a question as to the patriotism of the great City of Chicago and the State of Illinois. We are for the American Legion first, last, and all the time, and I will pledge Illinois' seven hundred thousand soldiers who have gone to the front for the colors in this organization to a man."

"... and clean its skirts of the stigma which is attached and we know you are going to help us in it, for we will have the support of the American Legion and with that support when the boys from over there get back, nothing will stop us from cleaning our skirts...."

Attention is drawn specifically to that sentence, because it affords an excellent opportunity to explain the difference between politics and policies. The Legion has policies but it is not political. One prime policy is the demand for one hundred per cent. Americanism. Whoever or whatever cannot read that mark, be it Chicago's mayor or the Seattle Soldier's Council, the Legion's caution is "measure up." The Legion, *as the Legion* will not go into municipal politics in Chicago but the members of the various posts in that city like all other Legion members stand for one hundred per cent, simon-pure patriotism and regardless of party, he who does not "measure up" had best beware. The Legion, as the Legion, never will endorse a political party or a party's candidate for office. But it will have platforms, it will have tenets, it will have principles. These platforms, tenets, and principles will be seen, felt, heard, and heeded by the voters of the United States. Furthermore, these platforms, tenets, and principles will be supported regardless of political party, political affiliations, or partisan sponsorship.

Chapter Nine - Objectors—Conscientious and Otherwise

The first of the committee reports of the morning was that of the Publication Committee. This report is perhaps not so interesting a document now as it may be in later years, when, with a circulation of millions weekly, the official organ will be a tremendous power for Americanism throughout the country, spreading in every home, in every vale and hamlet the same dragnet of Americanism as the draft law did, having in its tentacles the same power for culture, breadth of experience, and abolition of sectionalism.

In view of this, the report possesses tremendous potentialities. Here it is:

"The Committee on Publication recommends that this caucus of the American Legion inaugurate a national publication which shall be the Legion's exponent of Americanism; that this, the sole and only publication of the American Legion, be owned and directed by the Legion for and in the interest of all Americans; that the Publication Committee be continued that it may proceed as organized with the details of founding this publication, with the advice and under the control of the Executive Committee of the American Legion which shall add such specially qualified members to the Publication Committee as it may see fit; that this publication shall be a National, nonpartisan, non-sectional organ for the service of the American people, a champion of Americanism which means independence, security, health, education, greater contentment, and progress for every patriot, to be the torch, the beacon light thrown into our hands by the Americans who fell, and held as a unique and living monument to that other legion which did not come back.

"(Signed) G.P. Putnam, *Chairman.*

"Charles D. Kelley, *Secretary.*"

As an aside it may be interesting to say that there were at least half a dozen publishers, some with veteran journals already started, in St. Louis with the most alluring offers. Each wanted to have his publication designated as the official organ. Several other propositions were made, one syndicate offering to publish the magazine, bear the entire expense, give the Legion fifty per cent. of the stock, and allow it to control the editorial policy. All the syndicate wanted was the official endorsement. From other quarters came the word that a million dollars would be forthcoming, if such a large amount was necessary, in order to start the publication, but those who would furnish it wanted some return, naturally. However the Publication Committee felt, as set forth in the resolutions, that the magazine must be entirely owned and solely controlled by the Legion. If it was worth a million dollars to anybody else, it certainly was worth conserving in every possible way for the Legion.

Again I am going to let the minutes take up the story. Some of the details which they give in the next few pages are illustrative of the interest and care which the caucus took when it came to important matters.

Secretary Wood: "The Committee on Resolutions begs to submit the following report:

"'General Principles and Creed—Recognizing the supreme obligation of the citizens to maintain our national honor and integrity, and being resolved that the fruits of the Great War shall not die, we who participated in the war in order that the principles of justice, freedom, and democracy may more completely direct and influence the daily lives of America's manhood, do announce our adherence to the following principles and purposes:

"'(a) To inculcate the duties and obligations of citizenship.

"'(b) To preserve the history and incidents of our participation in this war.

"'(c) To cement the ties of comradeship formed in service.

"'(d) To promote, assist, and protect the general welfare of all soldiers, sailors, and marines and those dependent upon them.

"'(e) To encourage the maintenance of individual and national efficiency to the end that the nation shall never fail in its obligations.

"'(f) To maintain the principle that undivided and uncompromising support of the constitution of the United States is the true test of loyalty.'" (Applause.)

The Chairman: "Do you desire to pass on that as read, gentlemen, or by paragraphs?"

Mr. Johnson (Rhode Island): "I move it be adopted as a whole."

Seconded by Mr. Black of New York.

Col. Herbert (Mass.): "I would like to ask for information: if there aren't more eligible to membership in the American Legion than are cited—soldiers, sailors, and marines?"

The Chairman: "The committee understands that covers everything. The direct eligibility comes up later."

Col. Herbert: "But before we adopt this we must know who are eligible so it may be inserted there. As I read the qualifications for membership the members of the enlisted nurse corps are eligible to membership in the American Legion. If they are eligible they must be included there. If there are any others they must be included."

Mr. Fish (of New York): "I make a motion to the effect that this report be laid on the table until the constitution has been adopted. There are points in this resolution that conflict with the preamble and by-laws of the constitution. I move you, Mr. Chairman, that the first paragraph of the resolution as read be laid on the table until after the constitution is adopted. I will amend my motion to that effect."

Col. Herbert: "I want to hear that reread."

Secretary Wood: "What I have read, and what I am about to read again, is the first paragraph of the report of the Resolutions Committee. There are many other paragraphs. The second one, for instance, is an endorsement of the Victory Liberty Loan. If you lay the whole report on the table we have to wait until later to consider resolutions as a whole. The first paragraph is as follows:"

Secretary read first paragraph.

Mr. Milligan: "I wish to make a further amendment that the entire report be laid on the table until after the constitution has been adopted. I don't believe it is the sense of this meeting to hear the report of this committee in fragments."

Colonel Lea (of Tenn.): "If this report, or any part of it, is laid on the table it means final disposition of it under the rules of the House of Representatives. I don't think we want to do that until the report is read. As a substitute for the pending motion and amendment, I move that further reading and action of the report be suspended until after the report of the Committee on Constitution and By-Laws."

Seconded by Mr. Black of New York and carried.

The Chairman: "The Secretary will now proceed to read the resolutions."

Secretary Wood: "Endorsement of the Victory Liberty Loan.

"'Whereas, The Government of the United States has appealed to the country for financial support in order to provide the funds for expenditures made necessary in the prosecution of the war, and to reestablish the country upon a peace basis, therefore be it

"'Resolved that this caucus emphatically endorse the Victory Liberty Loan, and urges all Americans to promote the success of the loan in every manner possible.'"

The Chairman: "What is your pleasure with regard to that resolution?"

Mr. Sullivan: "I move the adoption of the resolution."

Seconded by Mr. Wickersham of New York and carried.

Secretary Wood: "Conscientious Objectors.

"'Resolved, that this caucus go on record as condemning the action of those responsible for protecting the men who refused full military service to the United States in accordance with the act of Congress of May 18, 1917, and who were tried by general court-martial, sentenced to prison and later fully pardoned, restored to duty and honorably discharged, with all back pay and allowances given them, and as condemning further the I.W.W.'s, international socialists, and anarchists in their effort to secure the release of these men already pardoned, and those still in prison, serving sentence, and be it further

"'Resolved, that this caucus requests a full and complete investigation by Congress of the trial and conviction of these parties and of their subsequent pardon." (Applause.)

Colonel Herbert (of Mass.): "I move you, sir, that this convention substitute the word 'demand' instead of 'request' where it says 'We request Congress.' We are a body large enough and representative enough and powerful enough to tell Congress what we want (applause), not to ask it, and I move the substitution of the word 'demand' instead of 'request.'"

Seconded by Luke Lea of Tennessee.

The Chairman: "The motion is now for the adoption of the resolution as read, substituting the word 'demand' for 'request.'"

Albert H. Wilson (of Idaho): "Gentlemen of this convention, before this is put to the body of this house, I want to offer a resolution that the man who convicted these men at Camp Funston be permitted to give the facts of those convictions and the facts of those discharges to the body of this house. I refer, gentlemen, to Major Foster, of Camp Funston, of the General Staff at Camp Funston, and I offer a resolution to that effect. Will you hear him?"

Assent from the audience.

Mr. Gaston: "I second that."

The Chairman: "It isn't necessary to have a resolution to that effect. The discussion would be germane to the question before the house."

Major Foster (of Missouri): "Gentlemen, on May 18, 1917, the Congress of these United States passed an act defining what should be done in regard to conscientious objectors. That act, as you are all probably familiar with, says nothing about the I.W.W.—the so-called humanitarian, the slacker, and the anarchist, and yet for some unknown reason about 135 such cattle were shipped out to Camp Funston, segregated, were not required to do military service, were tried for disobedience to a lawful order in time of war, duly convicted, sentenced to prison, and a large Majority of them pardoned out of the penitentiary within two months.

"These men, and I want you to get the importance of this, are not ordinary, poor, misguided, fanatical men, but the large number of them were college graduates. Take the case of Lundy in Chicago and Berger and Greenberg and all of them. Seven of them were cases so serious that the court, of which I was a member, sentenced them to death. Within three weeks the order came from Washington restoring them to honorable duty. These men who were dismissed from Leavenworth and who were tried by this court made the statement before the court to prove their conscientious scruples that they did not accept pay from the Government, nor did they, but when they were dismissed at Fort Leavenworth and honorably restored to duty and given discharges with honor, they took every dollar and cent that the Government sent or the officials in Washington said should be paid to them and they carefully counted it and it amounted to between four and six hundred dollars each, and they went home with it.

"You all know who is responsible for this condition. You all know that this convention should condemn it. And here is one more point I want to put before you and I want you to get this carefully. One of the men we tried, Worsman, has been pardoned. Here is a letter he sent out. I will not read it all.

(The caucus requests him to read it all.)

It is sent out to the press and to everyone. Here is a book that has the expressions before the court that all these men made and they stand on that as being proper.

"This letter says: 'The committee who sends you this letter are, for the most part, near relatives or close friends of young men now serving long terms in the disciplinary barracks at Fort Leavenworth because of loyalty of principle. Nearly all of them are your fellow workers and except for those in what we call the religious group,—trade unionists—the public knows little of their unhappy fate, even less than the other political or labor prisoners because they have been sent to prison by military court-martials and some have not even had the hostile publicity of a public trial in court.

"'The war is over; whether these men were right or wrong, they were utterly sincere. Even military prejudice has to concede that, and the sufferings they have unflinchingly borne prove it many times over, but the point for the country to get just now is that right or wrong, they cannot now have any adverse effect upon the military policy of the Government to keep them in prison.' Here is the dangerous thing—'We are trying to educate public opinion, and particularly labor opinion, to the point where it will demand the release of these brave and sincere young men. We say "labor," because we know when labor really demands a thing, it gets done.' There is the dangerous thing, gentlemen, the direct connecting up of the I.W.W., the so-called international socialists and anarchists who were tried, convicted, and later pardoned by our War Department,—the direct connecting up between that element and those like the fellow who was sentenced to prison and who is sending out this letter, and this great and dangerous Bolshevism that is creeping into this country and is, I am afraid, more dangerous than many of us realize. I want to see this caucus go on record—don't be afraid—as strong as you can against this fellow. The officers who served on those courts know what we had to endure. We had to treat them respectfully; we were obliged to do that. Let me tell you a few things, if you don't know them, about what happened in the guardhouse among those men. They would not do a thing; they wouldn't make their own beds. They wouldn't flush the toilets in the guardhouse, and some red-blooded American soldiers had to go and pull the chain for them. I say you can't send out a message to these people too strong in condemnation of this type and of the action of the War Department or whoever is responsible for the solace and the protection that has been thrown around the man who hid under the cloak of an act of Congress that was designed to take care of the conscientious objectors, and there is no conscientious objector under that act except a man whose religious creed forbade him to take part in the war in any way. I thank you." (Applause.)

The Chairman: "Gentlemen, the question has been called. All those in favor of the motion as amended will vote 'aye.'"

The motion was unanimously carried.

The general comment at the time was that Major Foster's address summed up the opinion of the caucus on the War Department's action in regard to the objector, conscientious or otherwise.

The accusation that the Legion was being formed for political purposes has been frequently referred to in this account of the organization and there follows an instance which shows very clearly the attitude of the delegates toward anything that might tend to give to the caucus a political savor. Just after Major Foster's address the chairman held up his hand for silence.

"One moment before the next resolution is read," he said: "I am informed that one of the newspapers of St. Louis has circulated blanks among the delegates asking them to indicate thereon how they intend to vote in the next national election in this country. I would point out to those who are gathered here that this is a very improper suggestion and that the action should be repudiated by the men here filling out none of these blanks."

This statement was greeted both with anger and applause, the former at the paper's action, the latter because of the chair's suggestion, and Mr. Wickersham of New York made a motion that none of the blanks should be filled out and that no delegate should take part in such a poll. It carried unanimously and with acclamation. The blanks were not filled out and the men distributing them were ordered to leave the theater, which they did.

This is the nearest approach to a poll that took place at the St. Louis Caucus so far as I am able to ascertain. In fact it would have been quite impossible to take a poll except in the theater and I have been assured by men sitting in widely different parts of the house that no such poll was taken. The delegates' living quarters were in widely scattered parts of St. Louis and it would have been impossible to have got any large number of them together to take a poll except during the meeting in the theater.

Despite this fact, despite the motion of Major Wickersham, and its passage by acclamation, reports were circulated after the caucus, to the effect that a poll had been taken and that it showed so many votes for this man and so many votes for that one. The effect of that statement, while not doing widespread damage, caused the Legion leaders a great deal of embarrassment and a great deal of effort to correct the false impression among those not present at St. Louis to the effect that the caucus had a political complexion.

Following the refusal to allow a poll to be taken, the secretary read the following resolution:

"Whereas certain aliens during the emergency of the war sought to evade military duty by reason of their status as aliens, and

"Whereas, such an act indicates a lack on the part of such aliens of the proper spirit of Americanism, therefore be it

"Resolved that this caucus assembled urge upon the Congress of the United States the adoption of such measures that may be necessary to bring about the immediate deportation from the United States for all time of these aliens."

This resolution covered a subject very near the heart of Sergeant Jack Sullivan, the vice-chairman. He was on his feet immediately saying:

"I agree with the gentleman from Massachusetts, Comrade Herbert, that this is not the time to urge upon Congress but to demand of Congress and I offer you, sir, this as a substitute resolution:

"Whereas, there was a law passed by the Congress of these United States, July, 1918, known as an amendment to the Selective Service Act giving persons within the draft age who had taken out first papers for American citizenship the privilege of turning in said first papers to their local exemption board and thereby becoming exempt from service,

"Whereas, thousands of men within draft age who had been in this country for many years and had signified their intention to become citizens, took advantage of this law and thereby became exempted from military service, or were discharged from military service by reason thereof, and have taken lucrative positions in the mills, shipyards, and factories, and

"Whereas, in this great World War for Democracy the rank and file of the best of our American manhood have suffered and sacrificed themselves in order to uphold the principles upon which this country was founded and for which they were willing to give up their life's blood, if necessary, to preserve, and

"Whereas we, the American Legion assembled are of the opinion that these would-be Americans who turned in their first papers to avoid service are in our opinion neither fish, flesh, nor fowl and if allowed to remain in this country would contaminate the 100% true American soldiers and sailors who will return to again engage in the gainful pursuits of life. Therefore, be it

"Resolved: That we, the American Legion in convention assembled in St. Louis, this 8th, 9th, and 10th day of May, 1919, numbering millions of red-blooded Americans, do demand the Congress of these United States to immediately enact a law to send these aliens who withdrew their first papers and thereby avoided service, back to the country from whence they came, for we want them not, neither do we need them. The country which we live in and were ready and are now ready and willing to fight for is good enough for us and this country, which they live in and prospered in, yet were unwilling to fight for, is too damned good for them to remain in. Therefore, be it further

"Resolved, that a copy of these resolutions be sent to each and every member of the House and Senate of our United States and a copy be given to the public press."

"Respectfully presented

"(Signed) Sgt. Jack Sullivan.

"Delegate from Seattle, State of Washington."

"I move you, sir, the adoption of this resolution."

"Now, gentlemen, I have a telegram from Seattle which I will read. It is addressed to Jack Sullivan, St. Louis.

"'Executive Board American Legion of Liberty authorizes you to advocate before the St. Louis Convention as part of the Americanization program, that the organization bring its influence to bear throughout the United States to secure enactment by Congress of laws making it possible to deport alien slackers who avoided military service by renouncing their citizenship and signing affidavits that they would return to the country from which they came. A bill providing for their deportation introduced by Senator Jones of Washington failed to pass the last session of Congress because the demand for its passage from the State of Washington was not backed up by other States. Demand upon senators and representatives from their own constituents that a law should be passed to deport these slackers would probably result in action by the special sessions of Congress of nearly three hundred aliens who escaped military service in Seattle by renouncing their right to become citizens. Twenty-seven per cent, were shown to be I.W.W.'s of the thousands who thus escaped military service. Throughout the country a large percentage are probably of the element which is seeking to undermine American institutions. They still remain despite their affidavits that they would leave the country and there is no existing law under which they can be deported. The first move towards making this country one hundred per cent. American should be the elimination of aliens who are opposed to our Gov-

ernment and institutions and who poison the minds of others by their teach-
ings. Every senator and representative should be urged to back legislation
for the elimination of this element and we hope that this work will be adopted by the convention as part of the national program.

"'(Signed) American Legion of Liberty,

"'Norman E. Coles, *Secretary*.'"

" Jack " Sullivan of Seattle

First Vice-Chairman of the St. Louis Caucus

When Sullivan finished reading, he began one of the most stirring address-es made before the convention:

"Now let's not be afraid to put the cards on the table and say to the Con-gress of the United States that we are not afraid to trample on the toes of the diplomats of these alleged neutral countries who do not want legislation of this kind to pass," Sullivan plead. "We have the interest of the man who donned the khaki and the blue and when the ships bring the boys from over there, they must take back these alien slackers. We would be derelict in our duty to the boys who gave their all when they went over the top; we would be untrue to ourselves and the institutions and principles for which we fought if we did not see to it that these people were sent back.

"I was born in the State of Massachusetts and I was taught that citizenship meant something. As a boy I went out West where I learned that American citizenship meant something to the people of the West.

"To-day we are here from all parts of the country. We are not from any sec-tion alone, because we are all Americans, This is an organization of Ameri-cans. This should be a country of Americans and if our citizenship means something, the swine who come from other countries should be taught that it means something like what McCrae said:

"'When from failing hands we throw the torch to you,Be yours to hold it high;If ye break faith with us who die,We shall not sleep though poppies grow in Flanders' field.'

"Let's make this unanimous and do it now and say to the boys in Siberia and France that we are going to see to it when they get back here that those damned alien slackers are not going to be here, or if they are, they are going to be on the dock at Hoboken to go back to their own countries because they don't belong here and we are not going to allow them to remain."

Sullivan was seated amid prolonged cheering; it was his big slap at Bolshe-vism. When Colonel Lindsley restored order Colonel Ralph Cole of Ohio was recognized.

"The delegation from Ohio has authorized me to second this motion," he said. "This seems to be a unanimous caucus. There is harmony here. The most impressive fact in relation to this assembly is the militant spirit of Americanism that has been manifested. I chanced to be Assistant Adjutant of the 37th Division when the time came for the naturalization of aliens who were in the American Army. Thousands and thousands of young aliens came up and raised up their right hand and pledged fidelity to the American Con-stitution, and to fight for the supremacy of the American flag, but, there was a certain small element, a certain small percentage that refused to take the oath of allegiance and they appealed to the Constitution and their rights un-der the law and they were exempted from military service. And I say to you, gentlemen of this convention, any alien that will appeal to the law in order to avoid military duty has no right to the opportunity of peace in America." Here there was prolonged applause.

Chaplain J. W. Inzer of Alabama

"There was an outbreak in the State of Ohio of Bolshevism a few days ago, but I want you gentlemen to know that it was put down. It was hit by the soldiers who returned from France, the rank and file of our boys.

"Now, as Mr. Sullivan has suggested, let it not be said that when these boys that raised their right hand and took the oath of allegiance to the American flag return, that these contemptible skunks that demanded exemption under the law shall occupy the positions, which these truly loyal men should have. Let's give those positions to the returning American soldiers and the returning alien soldiers that fought for the American flag and helped us win the great victory." The applause given Sullivan was repeated.

Then the "Silver Lining," Chaplain Inzer, strode upon the stage. This time he was a very stern Silver Lining, and what he had to say he said with a vigor which characterized his speeches all during the convention.

"I want to offer an amendment," he said. "Mr. Sullivan's resolution does not cover the whole ground. As Naturalization Officer of the 14th Infantry, I happen to be observing enough to know that there are other men that ought to be included in this list. Often we called certain foreigners together who had been drafted and said, 'Now, men, we are going to go overseas in a short while. How long have you been in this country?'

"One said, 'fourteen years.'

"'How long have you been here?' to another.

"'I have been here so and so,' he answered.

"'All right, now,' we said, 'this has been your country. If we hadn't gone to war, you would have expected to be here.'

"'But we want to go home now.'

"'If you go home will you fight for your country?'

"'We don't know.'

"And they absolutely refused to take out citizenship papers. How do we know them? As Naturalization Officer I marked on every one of those papers. 'This man, though he has been here for four years or ten years refused naturalization in the hope that he might avoid overseas service.' Now, then, I move that we include in that motion that the files be gone through and every man who refused citizenship, who was a native of any other country, but adopted this country and refused to take out the citizenship papers we offered him, after he had been brought into the army by the draft, also be deported."

Before the applause began Colonel Luke Lea had the floor. He is tall and imposing and a powerful speaker.

"I want to see this made a complete and thorough job, and to that end I desire to offer a further amendment," he said. "We further demand the immediate deportation of every alien enemy who, during the war, was interned, whether such alien enemy be now interned or has been paroled. I merely want to say this: That any alien enemy who is too dangerous to be at large and bear the burdens of war, is too dangerous to be at large and participate in the blessings of peace."

This brought down the house. It was what everybody thought and wanted. It was what everybody had hoped for since the very first day during the war that the Department of Justice had made its first internments. There have been all sorts of stories telling about these interned aliens getting rooms with baths, tennis courts, swimming pools, and playgrounds, and everyone had consistently hoped that they would all be sent back to Germany or Austria at the earliest possible moment after the war. The same hope was expressed in regard to certain Scandinavians and Hollanders here who were active in behalf of Germany. One thing is certain and that is that none of the delegates present were opposed to this enemy alien deportation, or if they were they didn't or couldn't make themselves heard above the thunderous approbation.

Chaplain Inzer at this juncture jumped to his feet and heightened the applause by shouting, "There are four million men back of this organization. If I were a Bolshevik, I'd pack my grip and beat it."

The culmination of this particular phase of the caucus was most dramatic. A wounded soldier on crutches, and bearing two wound stripes on his arm, was helped to the stage beside the chairman. "I am Private Sossin of Kentucky," he shouted. "I was born and reared in Poland, and came to this country and began to enjoy all the freedom of the American Constitution when I was thirty-seven years old. I left my business and my family to fight for this country. And if any of my native countrymen are so despicable as not to want to fight for the grandest flag the world has ever seen, the flag which gives freedom to all who are oppressed, I say, damn him and kick him out of here so that we can show that we despise such slackers."

The Chairman: "All those in favor of the motion as finally amended will vote 'Aye.'" That "Aye" shook the theater.

The caucus then passed a resolution that every naturalized citizen convicted under the Espionage Act should have his citizenship revoked and should be deported.

Another telling blow for Americanism!

The caucus next went on record with a resolution calling for the protection of the uniform. Those firms and individuals who had used the uniform as a method of peddling their wares were scored in the resolution and it was the sense of the motion that everything possible should be done to prevent panhandlers and peddlers on the streets wearing the uniform of the United States.

The caucus also indorsed Secretary Lane's plan for the "Reclamation of arid, swamp, and cut-over timber lands." The resolution to that effect follows in full:

"Whereas, the reclamation of arid, swamp, and cut-over timber lands is one of the great constructive problems of immediate interest to the nation; and

"Whereas, one of the questions for immediate consideration is that of presenting to discharged soldiers and sailors an opportunity to establish homes and create for themselves a place in the field of constructive effort; and

"Whereas, one of the purposes for which the formation of the American Legion is contemplated is to take an energetic interest in all constructive measures designed to promote the happiness and contentment of the people, and to actively encourage all proper movements of a general nature to assist the men of the army and navy in solving the problems of wholesome existence; and

"Whereas, the Department of the Interior and the Reclamation Service have been engaged in formulating and presenting to the country broad, constructive plans for the reclamation of arid, swamp, and cut-over timber lands:

"Now, Therefore, Be It Resolved: By the caucus of delegates of the American Legion in convention assembled, in the City of Saint Louis, Missouri, that we endorse the efforts heretofore made for the reclamation of lands, and we respectfully urge upon the Congress of the United States the adoption at an early date of broad and comprehensive legislation for economic reclamation of all lands susceptible of reclamation and production."

Chapter Ten - The Re-Employment Problem

We are now coming to the consideration of a subject that was nearer to the heart of every delegate than any other. That is the reëmployment of one-time service men. This matter is of the most intimate and direct concern to the Legion and its leaders and because of its importance I believe the details of the discussion are sufficiently interesting to permit me to quote them verbatim from the minutes.

The Chairman: "The secretary will read the next resolution."

Secretary Wood: "Reëmployment of ex-service men."

"Whereas, one of the most important questions of readjustment and reconstruction is the question of employment of the returning and returned soldiers, and

"Whereas, no principle is more sound than that growing out of the general patriotic attitude toward the returning soldier, vouchsafing to him return to his former employment or to a better job, therefore, be it

"Resolved: That the American Legion in its first national caucus assembled, declares to the people of the United States that no act can be more unpatriotic in these most serious days of readjustment and reconstruction than the violation of this principle announced which pledges immediate reemployment to the returned soldiers, and be it further

"Resolved: That the American Legion in its national caucus assembled does hereby declare itself as supporting in every proper way the efforts of the ex-service men to secure reemployment, and recommends that simple patriotism requires that ex-soldiers or ex-sailors and ex-marines be given preference whenever additional men are to be employed in any private or public enterprise, and be it further

"Resolved: That the American Legion recommends to Congress the prompt enactment of a program for internal improvement, having in view the necessity therefor and as an incident the absorption of the surplus labor of the country, giving preference to discharged ex-service men."

Mr. Walsh (Pittsburgh): "I move, Mr. Chairman, that we adopt the resolution."

The motion was seconded by Colonel Jones, of Washington, D.C.

Mr. Leveree: "Mr. Chairman and Gentlemen of the Convention, I desire to present to you a substitute for this resolution. As one who has been endeavoring to give a post-war service to these men who are coming back here and need to be replaced in the industries of this country, as a volunteer dollar-a-year man in the United States Employment Service and one who has accomplished results in the work to the extent that the bulletin of the National Chamber of Commerce has commented on the work, I desire to call your attention to the fact that the resolution as presented is not concrete. It says nothing. It talks in generalities, and I want to present to you a concrete proposition based on the experience of the Bureau in New Orleans."

"Whereas, it is desirable both for the welfare of the soldiers, sailors, and marines, now rapidly being discharged from the service of the United States of America, and for the industrial readjustment of the country that the process of returning these men to productive occupations in civil life be speeded up as much as possible;

"And Whereas, by reason of the failure of the Congress of the United States to appropriate funds for the purpose the said process has been retarded and left to private initiative; now, therefore, be it

"Resolved: That the American Legion in caucus assembled calls upon the Congress of the United States to promptly appropriate funds to be administered for the benefit of existing coordinated Bureaus for the Employment of Returning Soldiers, Sailors, and Marines, to the end that there may be no interruption in the service now being rendered and that it may be broadened and speeded up, be it further

"Resolved: That each local post or organization of the American Legion is urged during the period of demobilization to constitute itself a committee of the whole, which shall cooperate with the local Employment Bureau and shall establish and maintain a liaison between such Bureau and every employer in the community through members of the local post or organization who are already employed in such establishment to the end that it may be made easy for the employer to avail himself of the service of the Bureau by communicating with someone in his own establishment, and that every soldier, sailor, and marine already replaced in industry may have an opportunity to assist his comrades to become likewise."

"Gentlemen, this is the crux of that whole business—getting somebody close to the employer where you can bring about that liaison which is suggested in this substitute motion."

The motion to adopt the substitute resolution was made by Mr. Leveree and seconded by Mr. Luss.

Mr. Desmond (of Pennsylvania): "What has been said, in my estimation, is not comprehensive enough. In the city of Philadelphia which is known as the Cradle of Liberty, when the men who had given up positions in the educational system—I mean teachers—returned from the service of their country they were not, as promised, given the exact positions which they left. Neither were they given positions of parallel importance. They were actually demoted in grade so that these motions do not cover such circumstances. In many cases, in municipalities, men have returned from the service and have been forced to take positions not of a parallel grade but positions of a lower grade.

"Men, Americanism depends on America's school systems, and if the ones who are directing our school systems are so unpatriotic as to demote those who go forth to serve their country, what is going to become of America and Americanism? And I wish to make an amendment to the effect that municipalities and boards of education in those municipalities be forced to give men their parallel positions if not positions of better grade and that in no instance will they be allowed to demote a man because he has gone forth to serve his country. I put that forward as an amendment, that the municipal governments and boards of education in our municipalities be forced to give men positions of equal grade if they cannot give better grade."

Mr. Simington (of Washington): "I speak in opposition to that amended resolution. In my State I represent ten thousand organized men. In my State the present system has proven a failure. The organization that I represent handles an employment bureau that places 350 service men a week in permanent positions and 150 in temporary employment, and I say to you that that record is far and above the record of the U.S. Replacement Bureau. It is a proven failure. Gentlemen, I believe that it is 'For George to do'—and we are George.

"The service man wishes to take care of himself and his own. It is for the service man to handle his own problems and I suggest as an amendment—I am not sure of my being in order in offering an amendment to an amended amendment, but I suggest that it be the sense of this meeting that Congress assist the American Legion in taking care of its own in the matter of employment and that it do not use civilians to do the work." (Applause.)

The motion was seconded.

Mr. Hill (of Pennsylvania): "The original resolution that is before the convention, I am frank to say, has been forwarded to me by a soldier from Allegheny County, who walked the streets of Pittsburgh for eight or nine weeks pleading this principle. A resolution adopted by the Mothers of Democracy was sufficient for him to get back his job, because he held a position as a county employee of Allegheny County and he invoked this principle and vitalized every military organization in Allegheny County, and by means of that he got back his job and his back salary and his mother's allowance which was cut off since January 1, 1918. This resolution was originally presented by me as a member of the National Resolutions Committee from the State of Pennsylvania. The National Resolutions Committee appointed a subcommittee of which I was a member, a committee of three, to consider this and refer it back to the National Resolutions Committee. That committee passed favorably upon it and the National Resolutions Committee passed it.

"Now, if that resolution, as it stands before the house, was sufficient to get a job back for him, playing almost a lone hand, surely it is sufficient for any man here or for, this American Legion, for all it provides for, and all that is necessary to be done is the simple patriotism with the American Legion in back of it which can place its hands on the shoulder of any substantial employer and say, 'Do you wish to rectify yourself on this thing called "patriotism?"' Do you wish to give the soldier back his job who presents to you a meritorious case? We give you a chance. If you do not take it we will publish this thing and you will go down to contumely and stultification."

Mr. Knox: "Gentlemen, I am speaking on behalf of the Resolutions Committee. We spent all day yesterday listening to such requests as this. Our final calculated judgment is represented in the resolutions as presented. We found in the discussion that there was opposition to an endorsement of the United States Federal replacement division. (Applause.) And so we determined that the language as adopted covered the cast. We proposed to create in this organization a reemployment bureau of our own, and the resolution as presented is all the support that bureau needs.

"I move you, sir, that all the substitutes for the original resolution be laid on the table."

The motion was seconded.

Mr. Bennett Clark: "I simply want to call attention to the fact that under the rules of the House of Representatives that if you lay all amendments on the table it carries the entire proposition to the table and I don't believe this convention wants to do that."

Mr. Knox: "I ask a ruling on that, Mr. Chairman. If we lay all these substitutes for this resolution on the table will that kill the resolution?"

The Chairman: "Unless you dispense with the rules."

MR. KNOX: "Mr. Chairman, I move you, sir, the suspension of the rules to a sufficient extent so that we may table the substitutes which have been offered to the original resolution offered by the committee."

Motion seconded by Mr. Bond of New York and carried.

The Chairman: "The question now comes back to the original resolution."

The question was called for and it was adopted.

Mr. Ackley: "Mr. Chairman, I have another amendment to offer."

The Chairman: "It's too late. The secretary will read the next resolution."

Chapter Eleven - The Disregard of Self

I feel almost as if the next matter under discussion should have not only a special chapter devoted to it but be printed in large type and in distinctive ink, for I do not believe that anything so thoroughly gave evidence of the utter disregard of self in the Legion as did the flat refusal of the delegates to tolerate what has been called in some quarters, the "Pay Grab."

The minutes read:

Secretary Wood (Reading): "ADDITIONAL PAY FOR ENLISTED MEN."

"Whereas, the financial sacrifice of the enlisted persons in the military and naval service of the United States in the world war was altogether in excess of that of any other class of our citizenship, and

"Whereas, the great majority of these persons left lucrative employment upon joining the colors, and

"Whereas, this direct financial sacrifice was made at a time when men, many of them aliens who thrived in safety at home, were enjoying the advantages of an exceptionally high war wage, and

"Whereas, the service which involved this sacrifice was a Federal service in defense of our national honor and national security, therefore be it

"Resolved: That the delegates to this caucus of those who served with the colors in the world war urge upon the members of the 66th Congress the justice and propriety of appropriating a sufficient sum from the National Treasury to pay every person who served in the enlisted personnel in the military or naval service for a period of at least six months between April 6, 1917, and November 11, 1918, six months additional pay at the rate of $30.00 a month, and to those persons who served less than six months' in the military or naval service between April 6, 1917, and November 11, 1918, the sum of $15.00 per month for each month so served. This bonus to be in addition to any pay or bonus previously granted or authorized and to be paid upon and subject to the honorable discharge of any such person."

Mr. Knox: "Mr. Chairman, I move the adoption of the resolution as read."

The motion was seconded.

Mr. Mcgrath (New Jersey): "I served in the navy, and I simply want to call attention to the fact that this resolution says that the money shall be paid upon the honorable discharge of the soldiers and sailors, but in the navy we are only released from active duty and I will not be discharged for three years, neither will any of the other three hundred thousand naval reserves. I therefore move that the resolution be amended to say that so far as the navy is concerned that the money shall be paid upon their release from active duty or their honorable discharge."

The committee accepted the amendment.

The Chairman: "Before I put this motion I want to make this suggestion to you, that this is a pretty serious matter that you are considering. It is for this caucus, of course, in its wisdom to determine that which it wants to do, but up to this time, it has assumed continuously a most splendidly high and patriotic and unselfish attitude toward this whole question. It has dealt immediately and fairly and positively with regard to employment problems, but I suggest to you that we ought to consider very carefully whether we want to go on record as a caucus, as provided in this resolution, and I would prefer not to put the question until you have considered it further."

Fred Humphrey of New Mexico
A Vice-Chairman

The action of the caucus was foreshadowed by the applause which it gave to Colonel Lindsley's caution. Fully a half dozen men jumped to their feet and waved their hands wildly demanding recognition.

Private V. C. Calhoun, of Connecticut and the Marine Corps

He is a Vice-Chairman

Colonel Roosevelt arose from his seat with the New York delegation, and Chairman Lindsley recognized him.

"Gentlemen, I want to draw your attention to one feature of this question," he said. The Colonel spoke very deliberately and very distinctly, reminding a great many of his auditors of his father because of the way he snapped his words out. "I heartily agree with what the chair has said so far. I want you to get this particular reaction on the matter and I want to relate to you a little incident that happened coming out on the train from New York. One of the delegates on the same train with me said that the conductor stopped and talked to him and among other things said, 'Young Teddy Roosevelt is up ahead. He's going out to St. Louis to try to get some of the soldiers together to sandbag something out of the Government!' *Sandbag something out of the Government!*" The young Colonel's frame shook with emotion as he repeated that sentence. "Do you men get the idea of what he thought we were trying to do? We want everything that is right for us to have, but we are not going to try to sandbag the Government *out* of anything; primarily we are going to try to put something *into* the Government. In thinking over this resolution think of that."

The cheer which greeted this suggestion was so resounding and the opinion of the caucus so positive on this question that Mr. Gordon of Connecticut, a member of the committee that framed the resolution, moved that it should be laid on the table.

The thunderous "Aye" which tabled this resolution might well be recorded in letters of gold.

It showed the utter unselfishness of the American doughboy, gob, and leatherneck. He had followed Colonel Roosevelt's advice: he refused to sandbag the Government out of anything, and this action gives the best possible basis for the procedure to put something into the Government.

In view of the action of certain newspapers, organizations, and individuals in advocating that six months' pay should be given to the returned service man, I wonder if there are not still a great many of them who are still puzzled over why the Legion refused to endorse this movement. There must be scores of them, dozens of them who were not present at the St. Louis Caucus, to catch its spirit and who have not carefully considered just what impression such a demand on the part of former soldiers, sailors, and marines would create on the rest of the country.

Why shouldn't six months' pay be given to every man who did his bit in the war with Germany? In the first place, these men who have returned from the war have begotten for themselves the utmost respect and affection from those who could not go. The civilian forms the majority of our people. Because of the esteem before-mentioned, he is willing to grant almost anything *within reason* to the service man who risked so much in defense of the country. It is to the interest of the service man to make the civilian population feel that he does not want to get something for nothing but that, rather, he would still prefer to give his best to the country in peaceful times in the same spirit that he manifested in war times—an utter disregard of self.

Had the Legion endorsed this resolution, the general consensus would have been, "There are the soldiers getting together to make demands. Their organization is nothing more or less than an association formed to get something out of the Treasury." Therefore, when the service men, as a unit, came to demand something vitally necessary for the good of the country, it is possible that they might be answered: "We have paid you in money and have your receipt and that will be all for you."

This Legion can, must, and will be an inspiration and a guiding spirit because it is composed of men who have been willing to sacrifice self for the good of the country. For that they have obtained the affection of their world and just so long as they are willing to continue to manifest that spirit will they retain that affection.

Chapter Twelve - The Closing Hours

The next resolution to be passed was that concerning "Disability Pay." That resolution, as passed read.

"Whereas, under the provisions of the existing law an obvious injustice is done to the civilian who entered the military service, and as an incident, too, that service is disabled, therefore,

"BE IT Resolved: That this caucus urge upon Congress the enactment of legislation, which will place upon an equal basis as to retirement for disability incurred in active service during the war with the Central Powers of Europe, all officers and enlisted personnel who served in the military and naval forces of the United States during said war, irrespective of whether they happened to serve in the Regular Army, or in the National Guard or National Army."

Then followed the passage of the War Risk Insurance Resolution. This read:

"Whereas, one of the purposes of this organization is: 'To protect, assist, and promote the general welfare of all persons in the military and naval service of the United States and those dependent upon them,' and,

"Whereas, owing to the speedy demobilization of the men in the service, who had not had their rights, privileges, and benefits under the War Risk Insurance Act fully explained to them, and these men, therefore, are losing daily, such rights, privileges, and benefits, which may never again be restored, and,

"Whereas, it is desirable that every means be pursued to acquaint the men of their full rights, privileges, and benefits under the said act, and to prevent the loss of the said rights, benefits, and privileges, therefore,

"Be It Resolved: That this caucus pledges its most energetic support to a campaign of sound education and widespread activity, to the end that the rights, privileges, and benefits under the War Risk Insurance Act be conserved and that the men discharged from the service be made to realize what are their rights under this act; and that the Executive Committee be empowered and directed to confer with the War Risk Insurance Bureau, that it may carry out the purposes herein expressed and,

"Be It Further Resolved: That it is the sense of this caucus that the War Risk Insurance Act be amended to provide that the insured, under the act, may be allowed to elect whether his insurance, upon maturity, shall be paid as an annuity, or in one payment; and that he may select his beneficiaries regardless of family relationship."

At the time of the caucus, Colonel Lindsley was director of the War Risk Insurance Bureau in Washington. In speaking to the motion to pass the foregoing resolution, he said that more than a year ago he and other officers in France felt that if there were no other reasons for an organization such as the Legion, it would be more than worth while to create one even though its sole function was to let those who served in the war know their rights about government insurance and if it saw to it that the general scheme was perpetuated.

"I am speaking particularly of the insurance phase of the situation," he said in part. "The United States Government to-day is the greatest insurance institution on earth. Thirty-nine billions of dollars of applications have poured in from over four millions of men; an average of practically $9000 per man is held throughout the United States and abroad, and over 90% of these men are insured. That insurance is the best in the world, because the greatest and the best and the richest Government on earth says, 'I promise to pay.' It is the cheapest insurance in the world and always will be because the Government says, 'As part of our contribution, we, the people of the United States, in this war, as a legitimate expense, will pay all cost of administering this Bureau.' So that the men who have this insurance now and those who have it hereafter will pay only the net cost. If there is any savings, they get it. So that for all time to come they have got the insurance cheaper than any other country except the United States can give them. I say that without any improper comparison with the splendid, properly organized institutions in the United States. It is simply this: That the people of the United States pay this cost of administration. By June 1st the policies of conversion will be ready to be delivered to those who want them. You will be able to cease term insurance, if you wish, and have ordinary life, limited payment life, or endowment insurance. You can have any kind you please, but the big thing, my comrades, is this: To retain every single dollar of this insurance that you can afford to carry. Don't be in any particular hurry about conversion. If your income isn't good—carry this message back to the boys throughout the United States—if their income at this time doesn't justify carrying higher priced insurance, retain that which they have got and throughout this country tell the men that those who have lapsed their insurance because they didn't understand its value, because it wasn't properly presented to them at the period of demobilization by the Government, for it was not, tell them they are going to have every right of reinstatement without physical examination.

"There is going to be no snap judgment on any man who served in this war who, because he was not able when he went out or didn't have the information or because he was careless or for any other reason didn't carry on his insurance. I ask you, my friends, and I think it is one of the important functions of this great American Legion that is born here in St. Louis at this time,

90

to see that the fullest possible amount of this government insurance is maintained. Every man that holds a government policy is a part of the Government more than ever before. I ask you to bear this in mind and it is going to be within your power to say yes and no to many of the great problems of the United States.

"I ask you to see that this great bureau is kept out of politics and that it is administered, in the years to come in the interests of those for whom this law was enacted, those who served as soldiers, sailors, and marines in this war and their dependents. I thank you for this opportunity of presenting this matter to you."

"... It is going to be within your power to say yes or no to many of the great problems of the United States."

The service men know this but coming from a man like Colonel Lindsley it is especially important. How are they going to use this power? What sort of a legislative program will the Legion have? The answer isn't hard to find by a perusal of the resolutions which were passed and by remembering that most important one which did not pass, viz.: the pay grab.

The next resolution occupying the attention of the caucus was that one relating to disability of soldiers, sailors, and marines. It reads:

"Be It Resolved: That the delegates from the several States shall instruct their respective organizations to see that every disabled soldier, sailor, and marine be brought into contact with the Rehabilitation Department of the Federal Board at Washington, D.C., and,

"Be It Further Resolved: That the secretaries of the various states be instructed to write to the Federal Board for literature as to what it offers to disabled men, and that the members of the Legion be instructed to distribute this literature and to aid the wounded soldiers, sailors, and marines to take advantage of governmental assistance, and that every effort be made by the American Legion in the several States to stop any attempt to pauperize disabled men."

The whole work of the Legion as outlined at the caucus is constructive and therefore inspiring. The reader will note from the last resolution that members of the Legion are to be instructed to distribute the literature of the Rehabilitation Department among wounded soldiers, sailors, and marines and to show them how to take advantage of governmental assistance; and also that every effort will be made by the American Legion to stop any attempt to pauperize disabled men.

A higher-minded, more gentle resolve than that, can hardly be imagined. All of us remember the host of begging cripples who were going the rounds of the country even so long as thirty-five or forty years after the Civil War. This last resolution means that such will not be the case after this war. I think that it would be safe to say that in nine cases out of ten, after the Legion gets thoroughly started, crippled beggars who pretend to have been wounded in the service of their country will be fakers. Mr. Mott of Illinois, in the discussion on this question, brought out the fact that there were approximately sixty thousand soldiers, sailors, and marines permanently disabled as a result of wounds, accidents, and disease incurred in the war, while approximately one hundred and forty thousand discharged men were only more or less disabled.

The final resolution was that copies of all resolutions passed by the caucus were to be forwarded to every member of the United States Senate and each representative in Congress.

Louis A. Frothingham, chairman of the Resolutions Committee, made an address in which he thanked the people of St. Louis for their hospitality and the War Camp Community Service for its aid. The War Camp Community Service sent special men to St. Louis under the direction of Mr. Frank L. Jones to cooperate with its St. Louis leaders in helping to make the delegates comfortable. Arrangements were made whereby delegates of small means could get lodging for twenty-five cents a night and meals at the same price.

Mr. Foss of Ohio introduced the following resolution of thanks which was passed standing:

"Resolved: That a standing vote of thanks be tendered to the War Camp Community Service for its active hospitality to the delegates to this St. Louis Caucus of the American Legion, which is in keeping with its splendid work through the war in extending community service to our American soldiers, sailors, and marines, and,

"Be It Further Resolved: That an engrossed copy of this resolution be forwarded to the national secretary of the War Camp Community Service."

In this connection it might be well to digress a bit and to say that War Camp Community Service functioned splendidly for the young men of our Army, Navy, and Marine Corps during the war, and as "Community Service, Inc." intends to continue caring for not only the doughboys and gobs it served so well but for an enlarged patronage. During the conflict, War Camp Community Service organized the social and recreational resources of six hundred communities which were adjacent to training camps, army bases, and naval stations, and also developed the same resources in thirty large communities dominated by great war industries, of which the industrial centers at Bethlehem, Chester, and Erie, Pennsylvania, are types.

I believe it is well worth while for every member of the American Legion to know something about War Camp accomplishment, and Community Service possibilities for each has a similar aim and goal which may be realized by harmonious effort on the part of community service branches and legion posts throughout the entire country.

The idea of War Camp Community Service, like all successful experiments, was based on sound truth and simple theory and proved to be far reaching in results. Communities were not told what to do; there was no cut and dried program, but rather each community received special treatment suited to its particular needs, temperament, and physical characteristics. The basic idea underlying this activity is to allow each one to express himself. No person or community has the same thoughts, manner of living or thinking, and entire communities, like individuals, are affected by their environment and the life which circumstances compel them to lead. An iron monger's stalwart frame may conceal a poetic-soul, while the frail body of an obscure clerk may enclose the spirit of a Cromwell. War Camp has helped a great many such men to find themselves. Community Service promises to do the same thing, for the war has given ample proof of the need of just this kind of service.

With the war gone, with thousands of young men thrown upon their own initiative and resources for both work and play, there is going to be a great need of proper guidance, companionship, and comradeship, unless a great many are to be overtaken by some madness like Bolshevism or in a lesser degree—constant and brooding dissatisfaction. The American Legion post, with its leaders, is going to fill a great need here. It will be some place to go where a man can meet his fellows of the better type, and, not only indulge in the pleasure of discussing former days but, better still, take an interest in present-day movements affecting his country.

Also, I feel that Community Service will have a great place in this same scheme: that it can take the former service man, lonely and seeking expression, just where the Legion leaves off and, with Legion ideals on Americanism and the duties of citizenship as a basis, can round him off in the softer, more intimate molds of life, so that between the two he may not be only an honor to his country, but to his family and to his God as well. Therefore, I believe Community Service will fall heir to the goodwill created by War Camp throughout the nation, that it will retain the best of the latter's tenets and will take its place as one of the great powers for good in the community life of this country.

At the final session, Major Caspar G. Bacon was elected treasurer of the Legion to serve until November 11th. Delegations appointed State chairmen and secretaries to carry on the work of further organization for the November convention.

During luncheon time of the last day there had been some fear expressed among certain of the delegates that the loyal foreign-born element in the United States might not thoroughly understand the Alien Slackers Resolution. In order to make that perfectly clear Chaplain Inzer, during the last hours of the caucus, called for a cheer for every foreign-born citizen who gave loyal service to the United States. A rousing one was given.

Then came the unanimous report of the Committee on Constitution and By-Laws and declaration of principles. It was passed upon, section by section. You will find it printed elsewhere in this volume, and you must read it if you would get a true view of the principles underlying the Legion. It is as plain as a lesson in a school reader. Any comment on it from me would be editorial tautology, so I don't want to say anything more than that its framing was one of the cleverest and most comprehensive bits of work done since the very beginning of the Legion.

On the question of eligibility of Americans who had served in other armies, Mr. Palmen of California, announced as a bit of information that an Act approved by Congress on October 15, 1918, provided that such men must repatriate themselves. "We must go before a judge qualified to give citizenship back, taking with us our honorable discharge and credentials to show that we were American citizens at the time we enlisted," Mr. Palmen declared. Mr. Palmen was with the Canadian Army for three and a half years. "This question has been debated and the public at large is much confused about it," he continued. "I am told all that I must do is to go before a judge and that I will immediately be made a citizen again with all the rights and privileges which that implies."

There was no "hero stuff" at all at this caucus, no names of heroes, as such, were mentioned. The name of the President of the United States was not called nor any member of his Cabinet nor was any reference made to them either direct or indirect. This was done to avoid the appearance of politics. General Pershing's name was mentioned once and that was during the discussion of the sixth section of the constitution which provides that "no Post may be named for any living person."

Major Leonard of the District of Columbia delegation obtained the floor and said that his delegation was in an embarrassing position because they had already organized a post and named it "Pershing Post No. 1." Major Wickersham of New York, stated that a number of posts were already in the process of organization in his State and that the names of living men had been adopted by them.

After all why not call these posts after living men?

Delegate Harder, of Oklahoma, offered the answer:

"With all due respect to the gentlemen who have already named their posts they are subjected, as are we to the action of this caucus," he said. "We know positively that in due course of time those names will be used, at least to a certain extent, politically. Let us find some other way to honor these men and make it impossible for the people of this country to get the idea that this is a political organization."

There you have it, the real reason. Delegate Harder was only one of the hundreds who not only wanted to keep the Legion out of politics now but for all time to come.

Mr. McGrath of New Jersey also took an amusing fling at article six. As originally drawn it stipulated that the local unit should be termed a billet. "I object to the word billet," he said. "It has too many unpleasant associations as those men who slept in them in France will testify. A billet meant some place where you lay down and slept as long as certain little animals would let you, and the American Legion isn't going to do that."

Just about this time the afternoon was drawing to a close. Everybody realized that a monumental task had been performed. Sleepless nights and nerve-wracking days had been endured. Many pocketbooks were running low. Everybody felt it was time to go home.

General Hoffman of Oklahoma obtained recognition from the chair as some of the delegates already were rising to leave the theater. "I move, Mr. Chairman," shouted the General, "that we extend a vote of thanks to Colonel Roosevelt and Colonel Clark and other gentlemen who have been associated with them and to the chairman of this association and his able assistants who have brought this convention to such a happy and successful close."

At the mention of Colonel Roosevelt's name departing delegates tarried and when Mr. Weinman of Louisiana moved adjournment, the house stood and with one accord began to cry, "We want Teddy," "We want Teddy."

Colonel Roosevelt walked to the center of the stage and raised both hands seeking silence.

"I want to say just one thing," he said. "I have never been so much impressed in my life as I have been by the actions of this caucus, actions of the various committees and in the way this caucus thought for itself and acted for itself. For instance it would receive resolutions from the Resolutions Committee, would think them over, would re-decide on them and would re-decide them right. I want to say in closing that the only thing I regret is that my father could not have been alive at this moment to see the actions of this body of Americans."

Mr. Healey of the New York delegation obtained the attention of the chair. "I make a motion," stated Mr. Healey, "that before this great caucus adjourns we should remain standing in one minute's silence as a tribute to the greatest statesman that this nation has ever produced—THEODORE ROOSEVELT."

Chapter Thirteen - Why the American Legion?

As I glance back over these pages I am impressed with the fact that only the preface of "The Story of the American Legion" has been written here. When the reaches of the years shall gather to themselves the last of the men of the army, navy, and marine corps of the United States during its war against Germany that story may then be faithfully told. So the truth of the matter now is that history is in the writing so far as the American Legion in its relation to the United States of America is concerned. That statement isn't in reality as platitudinous as it seems at first thought.

We have arrived at world importance in history. We have come to that as the result of our part in the world war. Our isolation is over. We are the cynosure of all eyes. Uncle Sam is the dominant world figure; his hands control the reins that are driving the world. He has the enemies which all the successful have. There are those who had, and haven't, and there are those who never had, and want; all desiring, all envying the power of the United States of America. This great power and position was gained primarily by one motive—unselfishness. Just so long as it is our dominant trait will we retain what we have gained. Just so long as we remain true to our innate principles, to the tenets of our constitution, will we retain world importance and world influence.

There is a wolf at the gates of civilized Europe. If he gets inside nothing can stop him from ravishing us. This war has bound us so closely to Europe that we are, in a sense, one and the same. He who strikes our brother strikes us, even though he be so far away that the distance is measured by an ocean. We must get over the idea that distance makes a difference. The Atlantic ocean has just been crossed in sixteen hours. Remember, thought travels even faster.

The wolf that I mentioned is a Mad Thought. He is Bolshevism. He has the madness because of hunger, a hunger not only of body but of mind; the century-long hunger of the Russian peoples for Freedom. Russia has run in a circle. From the autocracy of the classes it has arrived at the autocracy of the masses.

Then, too, all our European brothers are war worn; tired, tired nearly to death with struggle and sacrifice, and this is not a frame of mind calculated to help reseat reason in the world.

Why the American Legion?

One of our great bankers recently returned from an intimate study of affairs abroad. His name is Frank A. Vanderlip. In an address before the Economic Club in New York City he said that Europe is paralyzed and that our task is to save.

I give the introduction to his address as it appeared in the New York *Times*:

"Frank A. Vanderlip, who spoke last night at the Hotel Astor, at a dinner of the Economic Club, which was held for the purpose of hearing his story of conditions in Europe, whence he has recently returned, said that England was on the verge of a revolution, which was narrowly averted in February, when he was there, and the conditions on the Continent of Europe are appalling beyond anything dreamed of in this country.

"He said that the food conditions in Europe would be worse instead of better for a year ahead, because of the dislocation of labor and the destruction of farm animals, and that the industrial and economic outlook, generally, points to a period after the war, which will equal, if not exceed the war period in suffering and misery.

"He said that Italy was afraid to disband her army, because she could not employ the men and was afraid of idleness. He said that the differential, which had kept England preëminent in international trade, was the underpayment of labor, and that this differential was now being wiped out, forcing England to face tremendously serious problems for the future. He quoted a British minister as saying that means would have to be found to send six or seven millions of Englishmen out of the British Isles and closer to the sources of food production, if continental conditions continued long as at present.

"He said that the best printing presses in the world to-day, except those in Washington, were at Petrograd, and that they were turning out masses of counterfeited pounds, francs, marks, lira, and pesetas, so skillfully made that detection was almost impossible. He said that these counterfeits were being spent largely by Germans to foment Bolshevist propaganda.

"Spain would, he said, be the most promising country in Europe except for the labor situation there, which had brought it to the verge of Bolshevism. He said that the most perfect laboratory of Bolshevism in Europe outside of Russia was in Barcelona, Spain, which he said was ruled absolutely by a mysterious secret council, which had censored and fined the newspapers until they quit publication and had enforced its will in all matters by assassinations, which no one dared to punish.

"He said that America alone could save Europe and that its aid must be extended to all countries equally. He said that this was necessary, not only to save Europe, but to prevent an invasion of America by the forces threatening the social overthrow of Europe."

Why the American Legion?

There, at least, is one great reason.

Our men of the army, navy, and marine corps got a schooling in the practical Americanism which our military establishment naturally teaches. Those who were aliens by birth and those native sons with inadequate educational advantages learned a great deal by association with men of better types and by travel. These men can and will stem the insidious guile of the wolf, and, to aid them in so doing, the Legion has an active speakers' bureau under Captain Osborn teaching Americanism in every section of the country. These speakers, in helping to organize the Legion along the right lines, teach the Constitution of the United States and preach that remedial changes in this government can be brought about in only one way, and that is, constitutionally.

Why the American Legion?

America is safe from any real danger if she can keep everybody busy. Less than two weeks after the caucus, the national executive committee had in process of formation a practicable scheme to aid in solving the reëmployment problem. As time goes on this department of Legion activity will become more and more efficient.

Here is another answer to the question.

All through these pages the reader has found references to this question of reëmployment; to anti-Bolshevism; the protection of the uniform; the non-partisan and non-political nature of the Legion; unselfishness; disability pay for the reserve forces; war risk insurance; allotments and back pay; the care of disabled service men; one hundred per cent. Americanism, and the deportation of those aliens who "bit the hand that fed them." The story has dealt almost entirely with these questions because primarily and fundamentally they are The American Legion. This program is the most important in the United States to-day. It means the betterment of the most stable forces in our community life, not only of to-day but for the next forty or fifty years. It means the proper extension of the influence of the most powerful factor for patriotism in our country—the onetime service man. It does not mean patriotism bounded on one side by a brass band and on the other by a dressy uniform and a reunion banner. It means real patriotism in its broadest sense—a clean body politic; a clean national soul and a clean international conscience.

This is the final answer to the question which serves as the title for this concluding chapter.

The American Legion

LIST OF STATE OFFICERS

Alabama:
- Chairman: Bibb Graves, Montgomery.
- Secretary: Leroy Jacobs, Care Jacobs Furniture Co., Birmingham.

Arizona:
- Chairman: E. Power Conway, Noll Bldg., Phoenix.
- Secretary: Fred B. Townsend, Natl. Bk., Arizona Bldg., Phoenix.

Arkansas:
- Chairman: J.J. Harrison, Little Rock.
- Secretary: Granville Burrow, Little Rock.

California:
- Chairman: Henry G. Mathewson, Flood Bldg., San Francisco.
- Secretary: E.E. Bohlen, 926 Flood Bldg., San Francisco.

Colorado:
- Chairman: H.A. Saidy, Colorado Springs.
- Secretary: Morton M. David, 401 Empire Bldg., Denver.

Connecticut:
- Chairman: Jas. B. Moody, Jr., 202 Phoenix Bk. Bldg., Hartford.
- Secretary: Alfred A. Phillips, Jr., 110 Glenbrook Rd., Stamford.

District of Columbia:
- Chairman: E. Lester Jones, 833 Southern Bldg., Washington.
- Secretary: Howard Fisk, 833 Southern Bldg., Washington.

Delaware:
- Chairman: Geo. N. Davis, 909 Market St., Wilmington.
- Secretary: L.K. Carpenter, Du Pont Bldg., Wilmington.

Florida:
- Chairman: S.L. Lowry, Jr., Citizens Bk. Bldg., Tampa.
- Secretary: J.T. Wiggington, 818—15th St., Miami.

Georgia:
- Chairman: Trammell Scott, 97 E. Merrits Ave., Atlanta.
- Secretary: Louis H. Bell, c/o Service Record, 208 Flatiron Bldg., Atlanta.

Hawaii:
- Chairman: Lawrence Judd, c/o T.H. Davies & Co., Ltd., Honolulu.
- Secretary: J.P. Morgan, Box 188, Honolulu.

Idaho:
- Chairman: C.M. Booth, Pocatello.
- Secretary: Laverne Collier, Pocatello.

Illinois:

- Chairman: George G. Seaman, Taylorville.
- Secretary: Myron E. Adams, 205 Marquette Bldg., 140 S. Dearborn St., Chicago.

Indiana:
- Chairman: Raymond S. Springer, Connersville.
- Secretary: L. Russell Newgent, 518 Hume Monsur Bldg., Indianapolis.

Iowa:
- Chairman: Matthew A. Tinley, Council Bluffs.
- Secretary: John MacVicar, 336 Hubbell Bldg., Des Moines.

Kansas:
- Chairman: A. Phares, 519 Sweiter Bldg., Wichita.
- Secretary: Ike Lambert, Emporia.

Kentucky:
- Chairman: Henry DeHaven Moorman, Hardinsburgh.
- Secretary: D.A. Sachs, Louisville.

Louisiana:
- Chairman: Allison Owen, 1237 State St., New Orleans.
- Secretary: T.H.H. Pratt, 721 Hibernia Bank, New Orleans.

Maine:
- Chairman: A.L. Robinson, 85 Exchange St., Portland.
- Secretary: James L. Boyle, 184 Water St., Augusta.

Maryland:
- Chairman: Jas. A. Gary, Jr., Equitable Bldg., Baltimore.
- Secretary: Alex. Randall, 12 West Chase St., Baltimore.

Massachusetts:
- Chairman: John F.J. Herbert, 749 Pleasant St., Worcester.
- Secretary: George P. Gilbody, 3 Van Winkle St., Boston.

Michigan:
- Chairman: Geo. C. Waldo, Detroit.
- Secretary: Ryle D. Tabor, 312 Moffatt Bldg., Detroit.

Minnesota:
- Chairman: Harrison Fuller, c/o St. Paul Dispatch, St. Paul.
- Secretary: George G. Chapin, 603 Guardian Life Bldg., St. Paul.

Mississippi:
- Chairman: Alex Fitzhugh, Vicksburgh.
- Secretary: John M. Alexander, Jackson.

Missouri:
- Chairman:
- Secretary:

Montana:
- Chairman: Chas. L. Sheridan, Bozeman.
- Secretary: Ben. W. Barnett, Helena.

Nebraska:

- Chairman: John G. Maher, Lincoln.
- Secretary: Allan A. Tukey, 1st Natl. Bank Bldg., Omaha.

Nevada:
- Chairman: E.L. Malsbary, Reno.
- Secretary: J.D. Salter, Winnimucca.

New Hampshire:
- Chairman: Frank Knox, Manchester.
- Secretary: Frank J. Abbott, Manchester.

New Jersey:
- Chairman: Hobart Brown, c/o Fireman's Insurance Co., Broad and Market Sts., Newark.
- Secretary: George W.C. McCarter, 765 Broad St., Newark.

New Mexico:
- Chairman: Charles M. DeBremon, Roswell.
- Secretary: Harry Howard Dorman, Santa Fé.

New York:
- Chairman: C.W. Wickersham, 140 Nassau St., New York City.
- Secretary: Wade H. Hayes, 140 Nassau St., New York City.

North Carolina:
- Chairman: C.K. Burgess, 107 Commercial Bank Bldg., Raleigh.
- Secretary: Charles N. Hulvey, A.&E. College, Raleigh.

North Dakota:
- Chairman: R.H. Treacy, Bismarck.
- Secretary: Ed. E. Gearey, Fargo.

Ohio:
- Chairman: P.C. Galbraith, Cincinnati.
- Secretary: Chalmers R. Wilson, Adj. Gen. Office, State House, Columbus.

Oklahoma:
- Chairman: Ross N. Lillard, Oklahoma City.
- Secretary: F.W. Fisher, Oklahoma City.

Oregon:
- Chairman: E.J. Eivers, 444-1/2 Larrabee St., Portland.
- Secretary: Dow V. Walker, Care Multnomah Club, Portland.

Pennsylvania:
- Chairman and Secretary: George F. Tyler, 121 S. 5th St., Philadelphia.

Rhode Island:
- Chairman: Alexander H. Johnson, City Hall, Providence.
- Secretary: James E. Cummiskey, Crompton.

South Carolina:
- Chairman: John D. Smyser, M.D., 423 South Gargan St., Florence.
- Secretary: Ben. D. Fulton, 32 West Evans St., Florence.

South Dakota:

- Chairman: T.R. Johnson, Sioux Falls.
- Secretary: J.C. Denison, Vermillion.

Tennessee:
- Chairman: Roan Waring, Bank of Commerce and Trust Co. Bldg., Memphis.
- Secretary: W.R. Craig, Nat. Life and Accident Co., Nashville, Tenn.

Texas:
- Chairman: Claude B. Birkhead, San Antonio.
- Secretary: J.A. Belzer, Austin.

Utah:
- Chairman: Harold R. Smoot, Salt Lake City.
- Secretary: Baldwin Robertson, 409 Ten Boston Bldg., Salt Lake City.

Virginia:
- Chairman: Andrew D. Christian, c/o Ruy & Power Bldg., Richmond.
- Secretary: R.G.M. Ross, 508 1st Nat'l. Bank Bldg. Newport News.

Vermont:
- Chairman: H. Nelson Jackson, Burlington.
- Secretary: Joseph H. Fountain, 138 Colchester Ave., Burlington.

Washington.
- Chairman: Harvey A. Moss, Seattle.
- Secretary: George R. Drever, c/o Adj. Gen. Office, Armory, Seattle.

West Virginia:
- Chairman: Jackson Arnold, 111 Court Ave., Weston.
- Secretary: Chas. McCamic, 904 Nat'l. Bank of West Virginia Bldg., Wheeling.

Wisconsin:
- Chairman: E.F. Ackley, 226 First Nat'l. Bk. Bldg., Milwaukee.
- Secretary: R.N. Gibson, Grand Rapids.

Wyoming:
- Chairman: A.H. Beach, Lusk.
- Secretary: R.H. Nichols, Casper.

Constitution of the American Legion

As Adopted by the St. Louis Caucus, May 10, 1919

PREAMBLE

For God and Country we associate ourselves together for the following purposes:

To uphold and defend the Constitution of the United States of America; to maintain law and order; to foster and perpetuate a one hundred per cent. Americanism; to preserve the memories and incidents of our association in the Great War; to inculcate a sense of individual obligation to the community, state, and nation; to combat the autocracy of both the classes and the masses; to make right the master of might; to promote peace and good will on earth; to safeguard and transmit to posterity the principles of justice, freedom, and democracy; to consecrate and sanctify our comradeship by our devotion to mutual helpfulness.

ARTICLE I - *Name*

The name of this organization shall be The American Legion.

ARTICLE II - *Membership*

All persons shall be eligible to membership in this organization who were in the military or naval service of the United States during the period between April 6, 1917, and November 11, 1918, both dates inclusive, and all persons who served in the military or naval services of any of the governments associated with the United States during the World War, provided that they were citizens of the United States at the time of their enlistment, and are again citizens at the time of application, except those persons who separated from the service under terms amounting to dishonorable discharge and except also those persons who refused to perform their military duties on the ground of conscientious or political obligation.

ARTICLE III - *Nature*

While requiring that every member of the organization perform his full duty as a citizen according to his own conscience and understanding, the organization shall be absolutely non-partisan, and shall not be used for the dissemination of partisan principles, or for the promotion of the candidacy of any person seeking public office or preferment.

ARTICLE IV - *Administration*

I. The Legislative Body of the organization shall be a national convention, to be held annually at a place and time to be fixed by vote of the preceding convention, or in the event that the preceding convention does not fix a time and place, then such time and place shall be fixed by the Executive Committee, hereinafter provided for.

2. The annual convention shall be composed of delegates and alternates from each state, the District of Columbia, and each territory and territorial possession of the United States, each of which shall be entitled to four delegates and four alternates, and to one additional delegate and alternate for each one thousand memberships paid up thirty days prior to the date of the national convention. The vote of each state, of the District of Columbia, and of each territory or territorial possession of the United States shall be equal to the total number of delegates to which that state, district, territory, or territorial possession is entitled.

3. The delegates to the national convention shall be chosen by each state in the manner hereinafter prescribed.

4. The executive power shall be vested in a National Executive Committee to be composed of two representatives from each state, the District of Columbia, territory and territorial possessions of the United States and such

other ex-officio members as may be elected by the Caucus. The National Executive Committee shall have authority to fill any vacancies in its membership.

ARTICLE V - *State Organization*

The state organization shall consist of that organization in each state, territory, or the District of Columbia whose delegates have been seated in the St. Louis Caucus. In those states which are at present unorganized the state organization shall consist of an Executive Committee to be chosen by a state convention and such other officers and committees as said convention may prescribe. The state convention in the latter case shall be called by the two members of the National Executive Committee in that state, territory, and the District of Columbia, and shall choose the delegates to the national convention, providing a fair representation for all sections of the state or territory. Each state organization shall receive a charter from the National Executive Committee.

The officers of the state organization shall be as follows:

- One State Commander.
- One State Vice Commander.
- One State Adjutant.
- One State Finance Officer.
- One State Historian.
- One State Master-at-Arms.
- One State Chaplain.

ARTICLE VI - *The Local Unit*

The local unit shall be termed the Post, which shall have a minimum membership of fifteen. No Post shall be received into this organization until it shall have received a charter. A Post desiring a charter shall apply to the State Organization and the charter shall be issued by the National Executive Committee whenever recommended by the State Organization. The National Executive Committee shall not issue a charter in the name of any living person.

The officers of the local organization shall be as follows:

- One Post Commander.
- One Post Vice Commander.
- One Post Adjutant.
- One Post Finance Officer.
- One Post Historian.
- One Post Chaplain.

and such appointive officers as may be provided by the State Organization.

ARTICLE VII - *Dues*

Each state organization shall pay to the National Executive Committee or such officer as said committee may designate therefor, the sum of twenty-five cents annually, for each individual member in that particular state, District of Columbia, territory, or territorial possession.

ARTICLE VIII - *Quorum*

A quorum shall exist at a national convention when there are present twenty-five or more states and territories partially or wholly represented as herein-before provided.

ARTICLE IX - *Rules*

The rules of procedure at the national convention shall be those set forth in Roberts' Rules of Order.

ARTICLE X - *Amendment*

This Constitution is to be in force until the November Convention, when it will be ratified or amended by that Convention.

Resolutions

Passed by the St. Louis Caucus, American Legion

May 10, 1919.

1. Endorsement of the Victory Liberty Loan.

Whereas, the Government of the United States has appealed to the country for financial support in order to provide the funds for expenditures made necessary in the prosecution of the war and to reestablish the country upon a Peace basis; therefore, be it

Resolved: That this caucus emphatically endorses the Victory Liberty Loan and urges all Americans to promote the success of the Loan in every manner possible.

2. Conscientious Objectors.

Resolved: That this caucus go on record as condemning the action of those responsible for protecting the men who refused full military service to the United States, in accordance with the Act of Congress of May 18, 1917, and who were tried by General Court Martial, sentenced to prison, and later fully pardoned, restored to duty, and honorably discharged, with all back pay and allowances given them; and as condemning further the I.W.W.'s, International Socialists, and Anarchists in their efforts to secure the release of these men already pardoned, and those still in prison, serving sentence, and,

Be It Further Resolved: That this caucus demand full and complete investigation by Congress, of the trial and conviction of these parties, and their subsequent pardon.

3. Protection of the Uniform.

Whereas, it is recognized that the uniform of the United States is as much a symbol as the flag itself, and thereby entitled to fitting respect, and, Whereas, certain unscrupulous firms and individuals have taken nefarious advantage of popular sentiment by utilizing men in uniforms as peddlers and sales-agents, and,

Whereas, certain discharged men have so far forgotten the respect due the uniform they wear, as to use it as an aid in peddling goods; therefore,

Be It Resolved: That this national caucus go on record as being unalterably opposed to such practices, and,

Be It Further Resolved: That each state and local organization here represented be urged to do all in its power to put an end to this misuse of the uniform, which has always been worn with honor and for noble purposes.

4. Reclamation of Arid, Swamp, and Cut-Over Timber Lands.

Whereas, the reclamation of arid, swamp, and cut-over timber lands is one of the great constructive problems of immediate interest to the nation; and,

Whereas, one of the questions for immediate consideration is that of presenting to discharged soldiers and sailors an opportunity to establish homes and create for themselves a place in the field of constructive effort; and,

Whereas, one of the purposes for which the formation of the American Legion is contemplated is to take an energetic interest in all constructive measures designed to promote the happiness and contentment of the people, and to actively encourage all proper movements of a general nature to assist the men of the Army and Navy in solving the problems of wholesome existence; and,

Whereas, the Department of the Interior and the Reclamation Service have been engaged in formulating and presenting to the country broad, constructive plans for the reclamation of arid, swamp and cut-over timber lands;

Now, Therefore, Be It Resolved: By the caucus of delegates of the American Legion in Convention assembled, in the City of Saint Louis, Missouri, that we endorse the efforts heretofore made for the reclamation of lands, and we respectfully urge upon the Congress of the United States the adoption at an early date of broad and comprehensive legislation for economic reclamation of all lands susceptible of reclamation and production.

5. Reëmployment of Ex-Service Men.

Whereas, one of the most important questions of Readjustment and Reconstruction, is the question of employment of the returning and returned soldiers and sailors, and,

Whereas, no principle is more sound than that growing out of the general patriotic attitude toward the returning soldier vouchsafing to him return to his former employment, or a better job;

Be It Resolved, That the American Legion in national caucus assembled, declares to the people of the United States that no act can be more unpatriotic in these most serious days of Readjustment and Reconstruction than the violation of the principle announced, which pledges immediate reëmployment to the returned soldier; and,

Be It Further Resolved: That the American Legion in its National Caucus assembled does hereby declare itself as supporting in every proper way, the efforts of the ex-service men to secure reëmployment, and recommends that simple patriotism requires that ex-soldiers, sailors, or marines be given preference whenever additional men are to be employed in any private or public enterprise; and,

Be It Further Resolved: That the American Legion recommends to Congress the prompt enactment of a program for internal improvement, having in view the necessity therefor, and as an incident the absorption of the surplus labor of the country, giving preference to discharged ex-service men.

6. Disability Pay.

Whereas, under the provisions of the existing law an obvious injustice is done to the civilian who entered the military service, and as an incident to that service is disabled; therefore,

Be It Resolved: That this Caucus urge upon Congress the enactment of legislation, which will place upon an equal basis as to retirement for disability incurred in active service during the War with the Central Powers of Europe, all officers and enlisted men who served in the Military and Naval forces of the United States during the War, irrespective of whether they happened to serve in the Regular Army, or in the National Guard or National Army.

7. War Risk Insurance.

Whereas, one of the purposes of this organization is: "To protect, assist, and promote the general welfare of all persons in the Military and Naval service of the United States, and those dependent upon them," and,

Whereas, owing to the speedy demobilization of the men in the service, who have not had their rights, privileges and benefits under the War Risk Insurance Act fully explained to them, and these men, therefore, are losing daily, such rights, privileges and benefits, which may never again be restored; and,

Whereas, it is desirable that every means be pursued to acquaint the men of their full rights, privileges, and benefits under the said Act, and to prevent the loss of the said rights, benefits and privileges; therefore,

Be It Resolved: That the American Legion pledges its most energetic support to a campaign of sound education and widespread activity, to the end that the rights, privileges and benefits under the War Risk Insurance Act be conserved, and that the men discharged from the service, be made to realize what are their rights under this act; and that the Executive Committee be empowered and directed to confer with the War Risk Insurance Bureau, that it may carry out the purposes herein expressed; and,

Be It Further Resolved: That it is the sense of this Caucus that the War Risk Insurance Act be amended to provide that the insured, under the Act, may be allowed to elect whether his insurance, upon maturity, shall be paid as an annuity, or in one payment; and that he may select his beneficiaries regardless of family relationship.

8. Alien Slackers.

Whereas, there was a law passed by the Congress of these United States in July, 1918, known as an Amendment to Selective Service Act, giving persons within the draft age, who had taken out first papers for American citizenship, the privilege of turning in said first papers to their local exemption board and thereby become exempt from service, and,

Whereas, thousands of men within draft age who had been in this country for many years and had signified their intention to become citizens, took advantage of this law and thereby became exempted from military service, or were discharged from military service by reason thereof, and have taken lucrative positions in the mills, shipyards and factories; and,

Whereas, in the great world war for democracy the rank and file of the best of our American manhood have suffered and sacrificed itself in order to uphold the principles upon which this country was founded, and for which they were willing to give up their life's blood; and,

Whereas, these counterfeit Americans who revoked their citizenship in our opinion would contaminate the 100 per cent. true American soldier, sailor, or marine who will shortly return to again engage in the gainful pursuits of life; therefore, be it

Resolved: That we, the American Legion, do demand the Congress of these United States to immediately enact a law to send these aliens, who withdrew their first papers, back to the country from which they came. The country in which we live, and for which we are willing to fight is good enough for us; but this country in which they have lived and prospered, yet for which they were unwilling to fight, is too good for them, and

Be It Further Resolved: That we demand the immediate deportation of every alien enemy who was interned during the war, whether the said alien enemy be now interned or has been paroled.

9. Disabled Soldiers, Sailors, and Marines.

Be It Resolved: That the delegates from the several states shall instruct their respective organizations to see that every disabled soldier, sailor and marine be brought into contact with the Rehabilitation Department of the Federal Board at Washington, D.C., and,

Be It Further Resolved: That the secretaries of the various states be instructed to write to the Federal Board for literature as to what it offers to disabled men, and that the members of the Legion be instructed to distribute this literature and to aid the wounded soldiers, sailors and marines, to take advantage of governmental assistance and that every effort be made by the American Legion in the several states to stop any attempt to pauperize disabled men.

10. Espionage Act.

Resolved: That every naturalized citizen convicted under the Espionage Act shall have his citizenship papers vacated, and when they shall have served their sentence they shall be deported to the country from which they came.

11. Resolutions.

Be It Resolved: That copies of these resolutions be forwarded to every member of the United States Senate and to each Representative in Congress.

Legion Facts

What has gone before is the story of the American Legion in the making. Now it is a going, growing institution.

Because it will be of vital interest and importance to every one of the four million Americans who wore the uniform, the following information concerning the American Legion, in the form of questions and answers, is here given, as follows:

(1) *What is the American Legion?*

(a) It is the organization of American veterans of the World War.

(2) *Who is eligible?*

(a) Any soldier, sailor or marine who served honorably between April 6, 1917, and November 11, 1918.

(3) *Are women eligible?*

(a) Yes, those who were regularly enlisted or commissioned in the army, navy or marine corps.

(4) *When was the Legion started?*

(a) It was first organized in Paris, March 15 to 17, 1919, by a thousand officers and men, delegates from all the units of the American Expeditionary Force to an organization caucus meeting, which adopted a tentative constitution and selected the name "American Legion."

(5) *What has been done in America regarding it?*

(a) The action of the Paris meeting was confirmed and endorsed by a similar meeting held in St. Louis, May 8 to 10, 1919, when the Legion was formally recognized by the troops who served in the United States.

(6) *Are the organizations in France and America separate?*

(a) No. The Paris caucus appointed an Executive Committee of seventeen officers and men to represent the troops in France in the conduct of the Legion. The St. Louis caucus appointed a similar Committee of Seventeen. These two Executive Committees have amalgamated and are now the governing body of the Legion.

(7) *Who are the officers of this national governing body?*

(a) Henry D. Lindsley, Texas, Chairman; Bennett C. Clark, Missouri, Vice-Chairman; Eric Fisher Wood, Pennsylvania, Secretary; Gaspar G. Bacon, Massachusetts, Treasurer.

(8) *Where are the temporary National Headquarters of the Legion?*

(a) At 19 West 44th Street, New York City.

(9) *When will the final step in the organization of the Legion take place?*

(a) November 10, 11 and 12, at Minneapolis, Minn., when a great National Convention will be held.

(10) *Why were those dates selected?*

(a) Because by that time practically all of the men of the A.E.F. will be at home and will have been able to participate in the election of their delegates to the Convention.

(11) *Who were some of the men who initiated the formation of the Legion?*

(a) Lt. Col. Theodore Roosevelt, of the First Division; Col. Henry D. Lindsley, formerly Mayor of Dallas, Texas; Sgt. "Jack" Sullivan, of Seattle; Lt. Col. Franklin D'Olier, of Philadelphia; Ex-Senator Luke Lea, of Tennessee; Lt. Col. Frederick Huedekoper, of Washington, D.C.; Major Redmond C. Stewart, of Baltimore; Wagoner Dale Shaw, of Iowa; Lt. Col. George A. White, of Oregon; "Bill" Donovan, of the "Fighting 69th"; Major Thomas R. Gowenlock, of Illinois; Sgt. Alvin C. York, of Tennessee; Colonel John Price Jackson, of the S.O.S.; Lt. Col. "Jack" Greenway, of Arizona; Sgt. Roy C. Haines, of Maine; George Edward Buxton, of Rhode Island; Eric Fisher Wood, of Pennsylvania; Chaplain John W. Inzer, of Alabama; Lt. Col. David M. Goodrich, of Akron; Chief Petty Officer B.J. Goldberg, of Chicago; "Tom" Miller, of Delaware; Major Alex. Laughlin, Jr., of Pittsburgh; Major Henry Leonard, of the Marine Corps; Dwight J. Davis, of the 35th Division; Corporal Charles S. Pew, of Montana; General William G. Price, of the 28th Division; Bishop Charles S. Brent, Senior Chaplain of the A.E.F.; General O'Ryan, of the 27th Division; Stewart Edward White, of California; Private Jesus M. Baca, of New Mexico; General Charles H. Cole, of the 26th Division; Sgt. E.L. Malsbary, of Nevada; Lt. Samuel Gompers, Jr., of New York; Col. Henry L. Stimpson, Ex-Secretary of War; Lt. Col. Charles W. Whittlesey, Commander of the "Lost Battalion"; Leroy Hoffman, of Oklahoma; Lt. Col. A. Piatt Andrew, of the American Ambulance in France; General Harvey J. Moss, of the State of Washington; John MacVicar, Mayor of Des Moines before the War; Sgt. George H.H. Pratt, of New Orleans; Col. F.C. Galbraith, of Cincinnati; Corporal Joseph H. Fountain, of Vermont; Devereux Milburn, of the 78th Division; Lt. Col. Wilbur Smith, of the 89th Division; Sgt. Theodore Myers, of Pennsylvania; Col. Bennett C. Clark, son of Champ Clark; Robert Bacon, Ex-Secretary of State.

(12) *What did the Legion, do at its St. Louis caucus?*

(a) It demanded investigation of the pardon and subsequent honorable discharge by the War Department of convicted conscientious objectors.

(b) It condemned the action of the I.W.Ws., the Anarchists, and the International Socialists.

(c) It protested against certain nefarious business concerns who are employing men in uniform to peddle their wares.

(d) It recommended that Congress should take steps to reclaim arid, swamp and cut over timber lands and give the work of doing this to ex-service men, and give the land to them when it had been made available for farming purposes.

(e) It demanded of Congress the same disability pay for men of the National Guard and National Army as now pertains to those in the Regular establishment.

(f) It initiated a campaign to secure to service men their rights and privileges under the War Risk Insurance Act.

(g) It demanded that Congress should deport to their own countries those aliens who refused to join the colors at the outbreak of the war, and pleaded their citizenship in other countries to escape the draft.

(h) It undertook to see that disabled soldiers, sailors and marines should be brought into contact with the Rehabilitation Department of the Government, which department helps them to learn and gain lucrative occupations.

(i) It authorized the appointment of a competent legislative committee to see that the above recommendations were effectively acted upon by Congress, and that committee has been appointed and is now at work.

(j) It authorized the establishment of a bureau to aid service men to get re-employment; and of a legal bureau to help them get from the Government their overdue pay and allotments. These two bureaus are being organized at the National Headquarters of the Legion and will be in active operation by July 1st.

(13) *What else did the St. Louis caucus do?*

(a) It endorsed all steps taken by the Paris caucus, and adopted a temporary constitution which conformed to the tentative constitution adopted in Paris.

(14) *What does this Constitution stand for?*

(a) The preamble answers that question; it reads: "For God and Country we associate ourselves together for the following purposes: To uphold and defend the Constitution of the United States of America; to maintain law and order; to foster and perpetuate a one hundred per cent. Americanism; to preserve the memories and incidents of our association in the Great War; to inculcate a sense of individual obligations to the community, state and nation; to combat the autocracy of both the classes and the masses; to make right the master of might; to promote peace and good will on earth; to safeguard and transmit to posterity the principles of justice, freedom and democracy; to consecrate and sanctify our comradeship by our devotion to mutual helpfulness."

(15) *How does the Legion govern itself?*

(a) The Constitution provides that the legislative body of the organization shall be a national convention, to be held annually ... composed of delegates and alternates from each state, from the District of Columbia and from each territory and territorial possession of the United States.

(16) *How is the Legion organized?*

(a) It is composed of State Branches, and these in turn are made up of Local Posts.

(17) *What is a Local Post?*

(a) The Constitution states that a Local Post shall have a minimum membership of fifteen. No Post shall be received into the Legion until it has received a charter. A Post desiring a charter shall apply for it to the State Branch, and the charter will be issued, upon recommendation of this State Branch, by the National Executive Committee. No Post may be named after any living person.

(18) *How can I join the American Legion?*

(a) By filling out the Enrollment Blank on the last page of this booklet and mailing it to the State Secretary of your home state, whose name is listed below. If there is a Local Post in your home town, your name and address will be sent to the Post Commander. If there is no Post in your home town, START ONE, write your State Secretary for the necessary particulars. The State Secretaries are:

Alabama.—Leroy Jacobs, care Jacobs Furniture Co., Birmingham.

Arizona.—Fred B. Townsend, National Bank, Arizona Bldg., Phoenix.

Arkansas.—Granville Burrow, Little Rock.

California.—E.E. Bohlen, 926 Flood Bldg., San Francisco.

Colorado.—Morton M. David, 401 Empire Bldg., Denver.

Connecticut.—Alfred A. Phillips, Jr., 110 Glenbrook Rd., Stamford.

Delaware.—L.K. Carpenter, Du Pont Bldg., Wilmington.

District Of Columbia.—Howard Fisk, 833 Southern Bldg., Washington.

Florida.—J.T. Wiggington, 818 15th St., Miami.

Georgia.—Louis H. Bell, care of Service Record, 208 Flatiron Bldg., Atlanta.

Hawaii.—J.P. Morgan, Box 188, Honolulu.

Idaho.—Laverne Collier, Pocatello.

Illinois.—Name not received yet.

Indiana.—L. Russell Newgent, 518 Hume Monsur Bldg., Indianapolis.

Iowa.—John MacVicar, 336 Hubbell Bldg., Des Moines.

Kansas.—Ike Lambert, Emporia.

Kentucky.—D.A. Sachs, Louisville.

Louisiana.—T.H.H. Pratt, 721 Hibernia Bank, New Orleans.

Maine.—James L. Boyle, 184 Water St., Augusta.

Maryland.—Alex. Randall, 12 West Chase St., Baltimore.

Massachusetts.—George F. Gilbody, 3 Van Winkle St., Boston.

Michigan.—Ryle D. Tabor, 312 Moffatt Bldg., Detroit.

Minnesota.—Merle E. Eaton, care of Lee & Lewis Grain Co., 200 Corn Exchange Bldg., Minneapolis.

Mississippi.—John M. Alexander, Jackson.

Missouri.—Ed. J. Cahill, Service Commission, Jefferson City.

Montana.—Ben W. Barnett, Helena.

Nebraska.—Allan A. Tukey, 1st National Bank Bldg., Omaha.

Nevada.—J.D. Salter, Winnimucca.

New Hampshire.—Frank J. Abbott, Manchester.

New Jersey.—George W.C. McCarter, 765 Broad St., Newark.

New Mexico.—Harry Howard Dorman, Santa Fé.

New York.—Wade H. Hayes, 140 Nassau St.

North Carolina.—Charles N. Hulvey, A. & E. College, Raleigh.

North Dakota.—Ed. E. Gearey, Fargo.

Ohio.—Chalmers R. Wilson, Adj. Gen. Office, State House, Columbus.

Oklahoma.—F.W. Fisher, Oklahoma City.

Oregon.—Dow V. Walker, care Multnomah Club, Portland.

Pennsylvania.—George F. Tyler, 121 S. 5th St., Philadelphia.

Rhode Island.—James E. Cummiskey, Crompton.

South Carolina.—Ben. D. Fulton, 32 West Evans St., Florence.

South Dakota.—J.C. Denison, Vermillion.

Tennessee.—W.R. Craig, Nat. Life and Accident Co., Nashville.

Texas.—J.A. Belzer, Austin.

Utah.—Baldwin Robertson, 409 Ten Boston Bldg., Salt Lake City.

Vermont.—Joseph H. Fountain, 138 Colchester Ave., Burlington.

Virginia.—R.G.M. Ross, 508 First National Bank Bldg., Newport News.

Washington.—George R. Drever, care Adj. Gen. Office, Armory, Seattle.

West Virginia.—Chas. McCamic, 904 National Bank of West Virginia Bldg., Wheeling.

Wisconsin.—R.N. Gibson, Grand Rapids.

Wyoming.—R.H. Nichols, Casper.

What the Public Press Thinks

It is interesting to know what the press of the United States thinks of the American Legion. Practically every newspaper in the country honored the Legion with comment. In almost every instance it was favorable. Selection has been made of some of this comment—as much as is feasible to give here. It is of two kinds: first, what the press thought of the *idea* of the Legion, and second, what opinion it had of the Legion after it was launched at St. Louis. The first type of comment was made prior to the caucus in this country and the second, afterwards. Comment on both types was generally favorable.

Lest insincerity be charged let it be said here that there *was* some unfavorable comment. One New England paper was surprised that soldiers, sailors and marines were not clever enough to know that the American people would perceive their attempt, through this organization, to "drive a six mule team through the Treasury" and get pension and pay grabs. One Southern paper pictured Colonel Roosevelt returning from the St. Louis caucus, a defeated candidate for the chairmanship, with all hope of the future blasted, while one in Ohio said with equal accuracy and solemnity that "there is no need of such an organization at this time, now that the country is entering the era of peace."

But here is the comment. It comes from north, east, south, and west, and it is typical:

New York Times, April 10, 1919.—... It is a pleasure to know that Lieutenant Colonel Theodore Roosevelt, the worthy inheritor of a beloved American name, has called a meeting of soldiers and sailors at St. Louis. Lieutenant Colonel Bennett Clark, son of Mr. Champ Clark, is an associate of Lieutenant Colonel Roosevelt, in the plan for an organization of all our soldiers and sailors as the American Legion. These two gentlemen, associated in a patriotic movement, indicate by their names its common national purpose, apart from politics and partisanship. "A nonpartisan and non-political association is to be formed," says Lieutenant Colonel Roosevelt, "an association which will keep alive the principles of justice, freedom, and democracy for which these veterans fought." Justice, freedom, and democracy, without partisanship! The idea is noble. It should prevail.

Leavenworth (Kansas) *Post*, April 30, 1919.—... The character of the men of the American Army who are promoting it [the Legion] and the high ideals which it professes and proposes to maintain are a guaranty that it will be a power for helpful service in the common family of the nation.

The plan of organization sprang from the desire of serious and able men in the American Army to maintain the high ideals for which all of them have fought, to preserve the soldier comradeship and carry it over into civilian life as an element of broad helpfulness while keeping the record of the army free from the taint of selfish aims. It was also wisely intended to forestall by the creation of one big genuinely representative, nonpartisan and democratic body, the formation of numerous smaller organizations in various places by men intent on exploiting the soldier sentiment and the soldier vote for other than patriotic purposes.

New York Sun, April 11, 1919.—... The American Legion will do an indispensable service. We, who have lived up to the past few years in an agitation of protest against the pension grab must now make our minds over sufficiently to realize that in the new situation we run immediately into danger not of over-pensioning the veterans of to-day but of neglecting them.

The new organization must of course be nonpartisan and non-political. Precedent enough exists in the career of the Grand Army to make that clear. It should include and enjoy the guidance of the most influential military men. Politicians it will have at its service so long as it is well run and organized from within. Despite its proper political limitations, it should serve as the most salutary means to influence returned soldiers to cling to plain old Americanism, shed their martial acquirements and return to plain, praiseworthy citizenship.

Washington Star, April 10, 1919.—... The American Legion is to be welcomed as an agency for the promotion of the best in our national life. It will represent, with other things, the majesty of numbers. A great many men will be eligible to membership; and they will be young, and full of hope and purpose. And when they act together in matters within the scope of their organization they will represent a force to be reckoned with in the formulating of public policies.

Brooklyn Eagle, April 11, 1919.—Organization of "The American Legion" is going on rapidly in every State in the Union. Vast as was the mass of eligibles on which the Grand Army of the Republic could draw after the Civil War, it did not compare with the Legion's bulk of raw material. There will be a formal caucus on May 8th, at St. Louis, of a real representative character, in which it is said the enlisted men of the army and navy will have a majority. Lieutenant Colonel Henry L. Stimson, once Secretary of War, outlines the plan. He believes that this country's future hereafter is in the hands of the men below thirty years of age who fought this war. He trusts that the lesson in practical democracy afforded by military experience and the ideals of democracy emphasized by military enthusiasm may be kept permanently alive.

That this is the main hope of the more active organizers we have no doubt. Men like Major General O'Ryan, General Charles I. Debevoise, and Colonel Theodore Roosevelt and Colonel Robert Bacon would never think of making such a body a lever for pension legislation or an agency of politics. Yet the temptation to a divergence from the higher ideals is strong, and the rank and file may not be inclined to resist it.

St. Louis Globe-Democrat, April 11, 1919.—... Such societies, it has been proved, are never partisan. They are invariably exponents of broad-gauge patriotism. That they have great political influence in a high national sense is true, but they have never misused it nor ever viewed their mission in a narrow spirit. They preserve the touch of the elbow throughout life, but only as thorough Americans, devoted first, last, and always to our common country.

St. Louis is proud to be selected as the place for the inauguration of this admirable and undoubtedly perpetual society. All wars are represented by societies formed by their veterans, and all alike have been truly and broadly patriotic. It will be the same with the new order, whose membership will, on the strength of numbers called to the colors, far exceed any former parallel. This event will be a datemark in our patriotic annals and in the progress of the nation.

Syracuse (N.Y.) *Herald,* April 13, 1919.—It has been earnestly stated, as might have been expected, that the American Legion will be strictly nonpartisan. That much might be inferred from the circumstance that one of the leading associates of Roosevelt in organizing the Legion is Lieutenant Colonel Bennett Clark, son of the late Democratic Speaker of the House of Representatives. Colonel Roosevelt is sufficient authority for the assurance that the movement is neither partisan nor political. He calls it "an association which will keep alive the principles of justice, freedom and democracy for which these veterans fought." Viewed in that sentimental, ethical and patriotic light, it is a commendable undertaking. The American people will wish it well, and be glad to see it flourish....

Norfolk (Va.) *Dispatch,* April 9, 1919.—If the American Legion now in process of organization by young Colonel Roosevelt and his associates, clings to the principles of foundation and holds by the purposes proclaimed by its founders, it may become a mighty force for good in the land. It will be composed of several millions of comparatively youthful Americans, a large percentage of whom will be voters, while virtually all will have demonstrated their readiness to fight their country's battles with weapons far deadlier than bullets.... This assumes the legion will fulfill the part it has undertaken to play in the country's life. If it should degenerate into a selfish protective body, it will be worse than useless. But there is little reason to fear it will fall so far below its ideals while there is every reason to hope it will be a powerful factor in helping the country to find itself again.

New Orleans Item, April 14, 1919.—The American Legion through the tremendous influence and mighty power of 3,000,000 organized fighting men, is certain to shape and control the destinies of the nation in years to come to an extent of which the wise will refrain from even suggesting a limit. With the announcement by Lieutenant Colonel Theodore Roosevelt that the "Legion will be interested in policies, but not in politics," the opinion may safely be hazarded that the great political parties of the country are due to have new mentors, from whom they may be forced to look anxiously for their cues.

Primarily among the announced purposes of the Legion is the perpetuating of those principles of justice, freedom and democracy for which its members either fought or stood ready to fight. On the field in France or in the training camps at home, the millions of America's best manhood have learned intimately and well a new lesson of individual and national responsibility. Such lessons, at the cost they were obtained, are not to be forgotten or lost. The ideals of the fighting men of the states, producing the valor and the power which made the American Army irresistible, and the revelations by fire of new realizations and brotherhood and of world and national citizenship are surely to be felt in the calm, happier times of peace.

Philadelphia Record, April 10, 1919.—... If, as Colonel Roosevelt predicts, the membership shall eventually comprise 4,000,000 men who were in the military and naval service of the United States in the late war, it will have possibilities of power that must be reckoned with. But if, in the long life before it, the American Legion shall have no more to its discredit than is summed up in the history of the G.A.R. whose ranks are now so pathetically thin, it will have been a worthy follower of its fathers.

Paterson (N.J.) *Evening News*, May 7, 1919.—... The new organization starts its career deserving and receiving the good wishes of the entire country. The character of the men of the American army who are promoting it and the high ideals which it professes and proposes to maintain are a guaranty that it will be a power for helpful service in the common family of the nation.

Duluth (Minn.) *Herald*, May 24, 1919.—There is a great field for the American Legion, the organization of American veterans of the World War, and judging by the spirit of the recent convention and by the expressions of the returning delegates as reported in the press of the country, it is going to fill that field.

And the field that awaits it, and that it seems to intend to fill, is a field of a vigorous and aggressive effort to demand and enforce a strong and coherent and consistent Americanism.

Not the swashbuckling kind of Americanism—the chip-on-the-shoulder kind—the we-can-lick-the-world kind. These lads of ours are the last in the world to preach that fool kind of Americanism. For they—or at least those of them who crossed the seas and fought for liberty and peace on the other side—have seen in the case of Germany what that kind of nationalism comes to, and they are against it.

But there is a type of Americanism which is utterly free from the taint of militarism and jingoism, but that yet is even more dangerous to anybody at home or abroad who flaunts the spirit of America and defies its power. And unless the signs fail, the American Legion is going to express and embody and inculcate that type of Americanism.

Anaconda (Mont.) *Standard*, May 24, 1919.—... At St. Louis the members voted down all proposals for obtaining from Congress increases of pay for the soldiers and rejected all efforts to obtain canvasses of the members to ascertain their preference as to parties and as to presidential candidates. Everything was excluded which would tend to commit the organization to any particular party or any particular candidate. Young Colonel Roosevelt, son of the former republican president, and Colonel Bennett Clark, son of Champ Clark, former democratic speaker of the house, joined hands in the endeavor to keep partisanship and politics out of the organization.

Collier's Weekly, May 31, 1919.—A national convention of American soldiers and sailors in which no grievances were aired, no political axes ground, no special privileges or preferments demanded; where oratorical "bunk" was hooted down; where social discrimination was taboo and military rank counted not at all; where the past glories of war were subordinated to the future glories of peace and where the national interest was placed above all partisanship—that is something new under the sun. It was in such a convention held in St. Louis during the second week in May, that the new spirit of the American army and navy expressed itself articulately for the first time since the armistice was signed. The birth of the American Legion was attended by circumstances having a significance comparable with those surrounding the signing of a certain document in Philadelphia one hundred and forty-three years ago, come July 4th.

A brigadier general arises to "place in nomination the name of a man who—" and is cried down by doughboys with calls of "Name him! Who is he?" A proposal to give extra pay to enlisted men is unanimously defeated because, as Lieutenant Colonel Roosevelt put it, "we are not here to sandbag something out of the Government, but to put something into it." The invitation to make Chicago the next meeting place of the Legion is refused because "American soldiers and sailors don't want to go to a city whose mayor would be ashamed to welcome such a convention." A progressive Republican, son of a famous father, refuses the chairmanship to quiet suspicion of personal ambition, and the office goes to a Southern Democrat of whose party the gathering is in complete ignorance.

One of the convention stenographers said: "This is the funniest convention I have ever attended." We have an idea that there was an element of prophecy in her homely remark—a body representing more than four million American soldiers and sailors that makes so little political noise is likely to be about as funny to the conventionally minded politician as a bombardment of gas shells. This language of restraint in the mouths of organized civilian youth may prove to be a natural companion to the famous battle slogan of the A.E.F.: "Let's go!"

New York Evening Post, May 3, 1919.—... The true usefulness of a veterans' organization is not far to seek. Like the G.A.R., the Legion should maintain and develop the comradeship bred by the war. It can assist the unfortunate in its ranks; it can take care of the widows and orphans of soldiers, in so far as any inadequacy of public provision seems to make care necessary. The Legion can preserve the fame of soldiers and commanders, by erecting monuments, by seeing that histories are written, and by proceedings of its regular reunions. It can foster such a public recollection of the great deeds of the war as well as broaden and deepen American patriotism. Sherman remarked in 1888 that there was some danger that a peace-loving generation in time of crises "would conclude that the wise man stays at home, and leaves the fools to take the buffets and kick of war." This danger can best be met by just such an organization as the G.A.R., with its campfires of song and story. Comradeship, charity and patriotism—these should be the Legion's watchwords.

New Haven (Conn.) *Union*, April 16, 1919.—... Its more immediate task, as its promoters see it, is to help the members and the families of members who maybe in need of assistance. No comrade of the great struggle is to feel that he is forgotten and forsaken by the comrades who served the same great cause. Its large and more permanent duty is to spread the sentiment of patriotism, to set an example of love of country, and unselfish service, to keep blooming always in the soldiers' bosom the flower of sacrifice that springs from every soldier's grave in France.

Philadelphia Press, April 10, 1919.—The organization of the soldiers of the late war into a permanent body is inevitable and entirely proper.

Capper's Weekly, May 24, 1919.—The American Legion organized at St. Louis is the new G.A.R. and through its platforms the views of the soldiers who fought in France will be heard. It is already apparent what the trend of that sentiment is. Whatever military system this nation sets up, if it meets the approval of the two million men who served the nation in the Great War, it will be democratic in spirit and as far as possible in form. It will be an army in which the self-respect of the common soldier will be recognized. The returning soldier has no use for anyone living here who is not wholly American, and is for expelling the unnaturalized alien wherever found. Loyalty to the Nation is fundamental in the soldiers' view.

The Nation must safeguard itself and make a distinction between citizens who offer themselves and their all, and citizens who, for whatever reason, withhold some part of their allegiance. Brutal treatment of conscientious objectors is neither civilized nor necessary, but a differentiation is created by such residents themselves, and there should be corresponding differentiation in rights and protection. This is one of the subjects that the returned soldiers have at heart.

Post Intelligencer, Seattle, Washington, May 21, 1919.—... The American Legion will be a political force in the nation as it has a perfect right to be. No organization of its character is to be held together by the cohesive power of reminiscence. Something more binding is required, and that something will be forthcoming whether anyone outside the Legion likes it or not....

The American Legion will be made up of intelligent young men who will have a community interest and whose interest can only be furthered by united action. They will know that nothing is more transient than public gratitude, and they will assuredly not rely on it.

Rochester (N.Y.) *Times*, May 23, 1919.—At its first convention held recently in St. Louis, the American Legion unanimously voted down a proposal to seek increased bonus money for the soldiers.

At that same meeting, Theodore Roosevelt, Jr., refused to accept official leadership of the organization because he desired to allow no ground for any charge that he wished to utilize it to further his political career.

Such action by the Legion and by one of its most prominent members warrant its organizers in working to enroll all the men who served during the great war.

If this path is followed the American Legion will be a force for good in the country's affairs as well as a bond of fellowship among those who were members of the largest army ever raised by this republic.

Manchester (N. H). *Union*, May 27, 1919.—... In spite of all that has been written and said it appears there still remains some mistaken idea and prejudices concerning this organization. The purposes of the American Legion are:

1. To uphold and defend the Constitution of the United States of America.

2. To maintain law and order.

3. To foster and perpetuate a one hundred per cent. Americanism.

4. To preserve the memories and incidents of our association in the Great War.

5. To inculcate a sense of individual obligation to the community, state and nation.

6. To combat the autocracy of both the classes and the masses.

7. To make right the master of might.

8. To promote peace and good will on earth.

9. To safeguard and transmit to posterity the principles of justice, freedom and democracy.

10. To consecrate and sanctify comradeship by devotion to mutual helpfulness.

This is the program and platform of the wonderful organization whose potential membership is the four million and more men who wore their country's uniform in the war.

It is big enough and broad enough to admit every man and woman who joined the colors. If, as has been intimated, there are some few ex-service men who think they see in this tremendous movement something personal and partisan, they should take the blinders off, forget their unworthy fears, and come out into the open with their comrades, determined, as every man is who has already joined, that the American Legion will never be made the vehicle of personal ambition nor the creature of partisan purpose; but will be conserved to foster and promote only those high purposes which are so nobly defined in the language which is quoted above, taken bodily from the constitution of the Legion.

PITTSBURGH, *Gazette-Times,* May 29, 1919.—... In contrast with the Grand Army, the American Legion will embrace all sections of our land. Similarly it will be the private soldier's organization. Military honors will not count. Absolute Americanism is to be its dominating principle. With the dwindling ranks of the Grand Army there is need of such an organization. The Grand Army has long been a staunch bulwark of patriotism but time is doing its work. Others must soon take up where the veterans of the Civil War left off. Those of the new organization who saw service overseas possess a new vision of what America means. Because of their good fortune in going abroad they reaped an advantage over those who were denied the privilege, though entitled to no more credit. All who donned the uniform served. With an organization of such possibilities in numbers and all imbued with a patriotic fervor the safety of the Republic against the machinations of those who would tear down is assured.

Burlington (Vt.) *News,* May 29, 1919.—So far as actual results are concerned America gains little from the peace treaty. If, however, the American Legion measures up to the standard we believe it capable of, America will be the greatest gainer of all in the war.

Bridgeport (Conn.) *Standard,* May 28, 1919.—The statement that the American Legion is to let politics alone is good news to the people of this country who are looking toward this fine organization of American fighters to bring to our national life some of the spirit which chased the Fritzies back to the Rhine. The civilian public has a right to ask what are the aims of this new, and sure to be powerful, organization. Four million men are of its potential membership. These four million are to be found scattered in every city, village and hamlet in the country. They are to meet on terms of equality, officers and men. They know how to work together, how to undergo discipline for a worthy objective, and how to go over the top in action. It is good, then, to know that this new four million is not to be a political machine. We want no more of the mawkish of either fearing or catering to the "soldier-vote."

Only as a nonpartisan organization can the American Legion do its best work. Its able leaders know this. In a day when men are fast deserting unworthy party emblems to stand for what they think right, the soldier organization will have a wide influence.

We hail the Legion.

It had to come and it is coming strong and sure.

Good men are at the head of the column, and better men than those in the ranks exist nowhere in the country.

They are the pick of the best, physically best, in nerve and in courage, best in point of training, in discipline and best among all the nations who won the great victory.

There is still a fight in America. Democracy is never safe, only being made safe. Eternal vigilance is the price of liberty. Eternal vigilance without regard to fear or favor is to be the spirit of the American Legion.

Committees

EXECUTIVE COMMITTEE

Alabama
- D.W.M. Jordan
- John W. Inzer

Alaska
- Edgar T. Hawley

Arizona
- John C. Greenway
- E.P. Conway

Arkansas
- Joe S. Harris
- James J. Harrison

California
- H.G. Mathewson
- C.E. Palmen

Colorado
- H.A. Saidy
- E.R. Myers

Connecticut
- H.C. Meserve
- A.M. Phillips, Jr.

Delaware
- George N. Doris
- George L. Evans

District of Columbia
- N.C. Turnage
- E. Lester Jones

Florida
- Davis Forster
- J.T. Wigginton

Georgia
- Louis H. Bell
- J.G. Juett

Hawaiian Islands
- J.P. Morgan

Idaho
- E.C. Booth
- Frank Esterbrook

Illinois
- William R. McCauley
- Marshall Field

Indiana
- Robert Morehead
- C.F. Strodel

Iowa
- H.H. Polk
- John MacVicar

Kansas
- W.S. Metcalf
- Sidney Moss

Kentucky
- Henry D. Moorman
- D.A. Sachs, Jr.

Louisiana
- Allison Owen
- Ralph Michel

Maine
- Albert Greenlaw
- Arthur L. Robinson

Maryland
- H.F. French
- Wm.A. Huster

Massachusetts

- G.G. Bacon
- J.F.J. Herbert

Michigan
- Frederick M. Alger
- A.C. Doyle

Minnesota
- Harrison Fuller
- A.M. Nelson

Mississippi
- Alex. Fitz-Hugh
- Fred Sullens

Missouri
- Court P. Allen
- H. Stattman

Montana
- H.L. Blomquist
- C.E. Pew

Nebraska
- John G. Maher
- Ed. P. McDermott

Nevada
- E.L. Malsbary
- T.J.D. Salter

New Hampshire
- Frank Knox
- Mathew Mahoney

New Jersey
- D.B. Muliken
- P.J. Ehrhardt

New Mexico
- B.M. Cutting
- O.A. Larrizola, Jr.

New York
- Theodore Roosevelt, Jr.
- Louis Burrill

North Carolina

North Dakota
- J.M. Hanley
- G.A. Fraser

Ohio
- J.L. Cochrun
- H.W. Snodgrass

Oklahoma
- Roy Hoffman

- Ralph H. Berry

Oregon
- E.J. Eivers
- W.B. Follett

Pennsylvania
- Franklin D'Olier
- A. Laughlin, Jr.

Rhode Island
- A. Johnson
- R.B. Weeden

South Carolina
- H.B. Springs
- M.B. Berkley

South Dakota
- J.C. Denison
- Joseph S. Pfeiffer

Tennessee
- Luke Lea
- Harry S. Berry

Texas
- W.E. Jackson
- Rolland Bradley

Utah
- Baldwin Robertson
- Royal Douglas

Vermont
- H. Nelson Jackson
- Joseph Fountain

Virginia
- C. Francis Cooke
- Andrew S. Christian

Washington
- L.L. Thompson
- Russ Simonton

West Virginia
- John G. Bond
- Charles McCamic

Wisconsin
- James Ackley
- G.W. Strampe

Wyoming
- C.M. June
- L.A. Miller

American Army Association

- Hayward H. Hillyer
- William P. Norton

World War Veterans
- G.H.W. Rauschkolb
- John S. Siebert

RESOLUTIONS COMMITTEE

Alabama
- Matthew H. Murphy

Alaska
- James Hawley

Arizona
- Ed. M. Le Baron

Arkansas
- Fred N. Tillman

California
- E.H. Dibble

Colorado
- H.A. Saidy

Connecticut
- F.W. Carroll

Delaware
- George N. Doris

District of Columbia
- Charles E. Johnston

Florida
- Carroll Ford

Georgia
- Eugene Sibert

Hawaii
- J.P. Morgan

Idaho
- C.M. Booth

Illinois
- Marshall Kearney

Indiana
- A.C. Duddelston

Iowa
- H.H. Polk

Kansas
- W.W. Hollaway

Kentucky
- M.K. Gordon

Louisiana
- John D. Ewing

Maine
- Roger A. Greene

Maryland
- H.L. French

Massachusetts
- L.A. Frothingham

Michigan
- Avery Gilleo

Minnesota
- S.S. Smith

Mississippi
- Alex. Fitz-Hugh

Missouri
- H.C. Clark

Montana
- Sam Abelstein

Nebraska
- Hird. Stryker

Nevada
- E.L. Malsbary

New Hampshire
- Frank Knox

New Jersey
- E.A. Tobin

New Mexico
- Roy H. Flamm

New York
- Robert Marsh

North Dakota
- J.R. Baker

Ohio
- E.J. Rummell

Oklahoma
- E.E. Atkins

Oregon
- B.E. Leonard

Pennsylvania
- Fred Hill

Philippines
- Robert R. Landon

Rhode Island
- W.P. Shunney

South Carolina
South Dakota
- William G. Buell
Tennessee
- G.P. Anderson
Texas
- Charles R. Tips
Utah
- R.J. Douglas
Vermont
- Guy Varnum
Virginia
- John J. Wicker, Jr.
Washington
- John J. Sullivan
West Virginia
- John C. Vaughan
Wisconsin
- Robert Cunningham
Wyoming
- L.A. Miller
American Army Association
- Joseph P. McGlinn
World War Veterans
- Thomas H. Dempsey

CONSTITUTION AND BY-LAWS COMMITTEE

Alabama
- Bibb Graves
Alaska
- James Hawley
Arizona
- John C. Greenway
Arkansas
- Burton S. Kinsworthy
California
- H.G. Mathewson
Colorado
- R. Dickson
Connecticut
- W.J. Malone
Delaware

- George W. Davis
District of Columbia
- John Lewis Smith
Florida
- J.T. Wigginton
Georgia
- L.H. Bell
Hawaiian Islands
- J.P. Morgan
Idaho
- C.M. Booth
Illinois
- C.G. Seeman
Indiana
- Scott R. Brewer
Iowa
- Fred M. Hudson
Kansas
- P.R. Johnson
Kentucky
- H.D. Haven Moorman
Louisiana
- Gus Blanchard
Maine
- Roy C. Haines
Maryland
- Wm. A. Huster
Massachusetts
- W.H. Howard
Michigan
- Howard Brink
Minnesota
- E.D. McCarthy
Mississippi
- Fred Sullens
Missouri
- Bennet Clark
Montana
- C.E. Pew
Nebraska
- L.J. McGuire
Nevada
- J.D. Salter
New Hampshire

- Frank J. Abbott

New Jersey
- Harlan Besson

New Mexico
- D.H. Wyatt

New York
- Hamilton Fish

North Carolina

North Dakota
- H.Y. Semling

Ohio
- J.F. Koons

Oklahoma
- Horace H. Hagan

Oregon
- Roderick D. Grant

Pennsylvania
- D.G. Foster

Rhode Island
- Percy Cantwell

South Carolina

South Dakota
- Wm. G. Buell

Tennessee
- Ed. Palmer

Texas
- Claud Birkhead

Utah
- R.S. McCarthy

Vermont
- J. Watson Webb

Virginia
- Wm. A Stuart

Washington
- L.L. Thompson

West Virginia
- Charles W. McCamic

Wisconsin
- Elmer Owens

Wyoming
- R.L. Powers

American Army Association
- Haywood W. Hillyer

ORGANIZATION COMMITTEE

Alabama
- Cecil Gaston

Alaska
- James Hawley

Arizona
- Alexander B. Baker

Arkansas
- Ross Mathis

California
- E.E. Bohlen

Colorado
- E.R. Meyer

Connecticut
- P.C. Calhoun

Delaware
- Irving Warner

District of Columbia
- Henry Leonard

Florida
- A.H. Blanding

Georgia
- R.L. Wilson, Jr.

Hawaii
- J.P. Morgan

Idaho
- Taylor Cummings

Illinois
- Frank Harrison

Indiana
- J.A. Umpleby

Iowa
- Maris B. De Wolfe

Kansas
- P.C. Stamford

Kentucky
- J.G. Wheeler

Louisiana
- Louis Ginella

Maine
- James U. Boyle

Maryland
- Wm. B. Wilmer

Massachusetts
- G.C. Cutler

Michigan
- J.F. Young

Minnesota
- Paul McMichael

Mississippi
- George Hoskin

Missouri
- F.L. Smith

Montana
- C.E. Pew

Nebraska
- Geo. H. Holveman

Nevada
- T.J.D. Salter

New Hampshire
- George V. Fiske

New Jersey
- R.P. Schenck

New Mexico
- Don. L. Blevins

New York
- Parton Swift

North Carolina

North Dakota
- J.P. Williams

Ohio
- L.J. Campbell

Oklahoma
- Hugh Haughery

Oregon
- J.L. May

Pennsylvania
- G.A. Rick

Rhode Island
- Alex. Johnson

South Carolina

South Dakota
- T.R. Johnston

Tennessee
- W.A. Shadow

Texas
- Arch C. Allen

Utah
- D.E. Rhivers

Vermont
- Leonard Nason

Virginia
- C. Brook Bollard

Washington
- Fred Redinger

West Virginia
- M.V. Godfrey

Wisconsin
- J.C. Davis

Wyoming
- Wm. Shortell

American Army Association
- Scott W. Lucas

World War Veterans
- Charles S. Watkins

CREDENTIAL COMMITTEE

Alabama
- Joseph Yates

Alaska
- James Hawley

Arizona
- F.P. Bernard

Arkansas
- Ivie Herschel

California
- B.W. Herhart

Colorado
- J.W. Gwin

Connecticut
- F.S. Butterworth

Delaware
- George L. Evans

District of Columbia
- S.P. Knut

Florida
- Davis Forster

Georgia
- J.G. Juett

Hawaiian Islands

- J.P. Morgan

Idaho
- Paul Peterson

Illinois
- Roger Young

Indiana
- J.W. Todd

Iowa
- P.M. Soper

Kansas
- I.E. Lambert

Kentucky
- Richard H. Slack

Louisiana
- G.H.H. Pratt

Maine
- Albert Greenlaw

Maryland
- J.S. Davis

Massachusetts
- G.F. Gilbody

Michigan
- H.A. O'Dell

Minnesota
- George Chapin

Mississippi
- John M. Alexander

Missouri
- D.W. Cronkite

Montana
- Doug. McCallum

Nebraska
- Orlando H. Kearney

Nevada
- T.J.D. Salter

New Hampshire
- John Santor

New Jersey
- C.S. Brady

New Mexico
- Jesus M. Baca

New York
- J.P. Goerke

North Dakota

- J.P. Williams

Ohio
- H.L. Bimm

Oklahoma
- F.W. Fisher

Oregon
- C.L. Mullen

Pennsylvania
- E.J. Pennell

Rhode Island
- F.B. Thurber

South Dakota
- T.R. Johnson

Tennessee
- J.D. Robertson

Texas
- John S. Hoover

Utah
- J.G. Wooley

Vermont
- Alexander Smith

Virginia
- G.R. Poole

Washington
- Fred Fein

West Virginia
- W.J. Simmons

Wisconsin
- M.A. Chybowski

Wyoming
- D.C. McCarthy

World War Veterans
- John S. Seibert

American Army Association
- H.W. Hillyer

COMMITTEE ON PERMANENT HEADQUARTERS

Alabama
- Beach Chenoweth

Alaska
- James Hawley

Arizona

- Alex. B. Baker

Arkansas

- Wm. Dougherty

California

- B.L. Shuman

Colorado

- D.J. Sparr

Connecticut

- B.R. Mathies

Delaware

- E.H. Kane

District of Columbia

- L. Clarkson Hines

Florida

- A.H. Blanding

Georgia

- Eugene Sibert

Hawaiian Islands

- J.P. Morgan

Idaho

- R.R. Wilson

Illinois

- Charles Wham

Indiana

- M.H. Thomas

Iowa

- Thompson L. Brookhart

Kansas

- W.A. Phares

Kentucky

- E.H. Marriner

Louisiana

- L.P. Beard

Maine

- Roger A. Greene

Maryland

- F.A. Young

Massachusetts

- W.H. Dolan

Michigan

- Wm. King

Minnesota

- D.R. St. Julian

Mississippi

- Robt. Burnett

Missouri

- A. Field

Montana

- Ben W. Barnett

Nebraska

- Geo. Gilligan

Nevada

- E.L. Malsbary

New Hampshire

- Arthur Trufant

New Jersey

- R.F. Ritter

New Mexico

- O.A. Lorizolla, Jr.

New York

- Thos. John Conway

North Carolina

North Dakota

- G.A. Fraser

Ohio

- J.L. Hall

Oklahoma

- Earl McNally

Oregon

- W.P. Follett

Pennsylvania

- C.A. Buettner

Philippine Islands.

- Robert Landon

Rhode Island

- Walter Sharkey

South Dakota

- W.G. Buell

Tennessee

- Ed. Buford

Texas

- Roy A. Jamison

Utah

- J.C. Kundson

Vermont

- L.H. Nason

Virginia

- Robt. P. Wallace

Washington
- C.B. McDonald

West Virginia
- Geo. S. Houston

Wisconsin
- James Pfeil

Wyoming
- C.M. June

American Army Association
- H.W. Hillyer

World War Veterans
- R.A. Thompson

COMMITTEE ON PUBLICATION

Alabama
- LeRoy Jacobs

Alaska
- James Hawley

Arizona
- M.E. Cassidy

Arkansas
- Roy Penix

California
- Clair Woolwine

Colorado
- W.E. Swink

Connecticut
- R.C. Vance

Delaware
- Irving Warner

District of Columbia
- Donald McGregor

Florida
- Conrad Ford

Georgia
- L.H. Bell

Hawaiian Islands
- J.P. Morgan

Idaho
- Paul Peterson

Illinois
- Richard M. O'Connell

Indiana
- Robt. Clee

Iowa
- H.D. Lemley

Kansas
- M.B. Musselman

Kentucky
- James G. Juett

Louisiana
- Rudolph Wienan

Maine
- Roy C. Haines

Maryland
- A.R. Hagner, Jr.

Massachusetts
- Donald Green

Michigan
- Chas. D. Kelley

Minnesota
- Jno. J. Ahern

Mississippi
- Chas. R. Dolbey

Missouri
- Robert Fullerton, Jr.

Montana
- Ben W. Barnett

Nebraska
- A.L. Stuart

Nevada
- E.L. Malsbary

New Hampshire
- C. Fred Maher

New Jersey
- Allen L. Eggers

New Mexico
- Jesus M. Baca

New York
- Geo. P. Putnam

North Dakota
- Arthur Gorman

Ohio
- H.M. Bush

Oklahoma
- W.T. Burling

Oregon

- B.E. Leonard

Pennsylvania
- Ammon Monroe Aurand, Jr.

Rhode Island
- Harry F. McKenna

South Dakota
- T.R. Johnson

Tennessee
- H.H. Corson, Jr.

Texas
- John W. Young

Utah
- Leo Meehan

Vermont
- L.H. Nason

Virginia
- D.D. Nei

Washington
- Russ Simonton

West Virginia
- Geo. S. Houston

Wisconsin
- C.M. Huntley

Wyoming
- Ralph L. Powers

American Army Association
- H.W. Hillyer

World War Veterans
- C.P. Dimmitt

FINANCE COMMITTEE

Alabama
- B.F. Stoddard

Alaska
- James Hawley

Arizona
- M.E. Cassidy

Arkansas
- Garland Hurt

California
- E.H. Dibbley

Colorado
- Ed. Krueger

Connecticut
- James B. Moody

Delaware
- Irving Warner

District of Columbia
- Howard F. Fiske

Florida
- Davis Forster

Georgia

Hawaii
- J.P. Morgan

Idaho
- John S. Green

Illinois
- Albert A. Sprague

Indiana
- Chester P. Wolfe

Iowa
- W.R. Hart

Kansas
- J.B. Brickell

Kentucky
- R. Ewall

Louisiana
- Levering Moore

Maine
- Waldemar P. Adams

Maryland
- Alexander Randall

Massachusetts
- J. Stewart

Michigan
- George M. Kesl

Minnesota
- O.H. Baldwin

Mississippi
- Paul Chambers

Missouri
- D.G. Hubbard

Montana
- Arthur Barry

Nebraska
- William Richie

Nevada

- T.J.D. Salter

New Hampshire
- William E. Sullivan

New Jersey
- Paul De Voise

New Mexico
- F.B. Humphrey

New York
- M.B. Murphy

North Dakota
- G.A. Fraser

Ohio
- B.J. Hard

Oklahoma
- William Viuer

Oregon
- C.L. Muffin

Pennsylvania
- James W. Gary

Rhode Island
- Jas. Elinniskey

South Carolina

South Dakota
- J.C. Denison

Tennessee
- Charles R. Bowman

Texas
- C.C. Beavens

Utah
- Harold R. Smoot

Vermont
- Pearl T. Clapp

Virginia
- J.T. Wyatt

Washington
- C.S. Sapp

West Virginia
- Clarence Jones

Wisconsin
- P.R. Minnahan

Wyoming
- N.V. Swensen

American Army Association
- Louis R. Florin

World War Veterans
- G.H.W. Rauschkolb

COMMITTEE ON NAME

Alabama
- Norman J. Reiss

Alaska
- James Hawley

Arizona
- Fred B. Townsend

Arkansas
- Roy W. Wood

California
- Clair Woolwine

Colorado
- Robt. G. Allen

Connecticut
- P.L. Sampsell

Delaware
- E.H. Kane

District of Columbia
- J. Bentley Mulford

Florida
- J.T. Wigginton

Georgia
- J.G. Juett

Hawaiian Islands
- J.P. Morgan

Idaho
- T.A. Feeney

Illinois
- Thos. Harwood

Indiana
- Augustus B. Wilson

Iowa
- Jackson R. Day

Kansas
- P.K. Cubbison

Kentucky
- W.O. Sayers

Louisiana
- Davis McCutcheon

Maine

- Waldemar P. Adams

Maryland
- G.H. Tieman

Massachusetts
- J.P. McGrath

Michigan
- B.B. Bellows

Minnesota
- W.R. Sturtz

Mississippi
- Arthur B. Clark

Missouri
- H.W. Holcomb

Montana
- H.L. Blomquist

Nebraska
- Frank F. Fischer

Nevada
- T.J.D. Salter

New Hampshire
- W.J. Murphy

New Jersey
- G.H. Stratton

New Mexico
- C.S. Caldwell

New York
- E.D. Bunn

North Carolina

North Dakota
- L.B. Merry

Ohio
- R.E. Shank

Oklahoma
- Robert B. Keenan

Oregon
- W.B. Follett

Pennsylvania
- B.L. Houck

Rhode Island
- Jos. San Soneitr

South Dakota
- T.R. Johnson

Tennessee
- Barton P. Brown

Texas
- Russ D. Langdon

Utah
- L.J. Seeley

Vermont
- Alexander Smith

Virginia
- Robt. R. Wallace

Washington
- Rob. S. Gordon

West Virginia
- Jas. M. Crockett

Wisconsin
- John P. Szultek

Wyoming
- Maurice Dineen

American Army Association
- H.W. Hillyer

SOLDIERS AND SAILORS COUNCIL
- S.H. Curtin

World War Veterans
- John S. Seibert

COMMITTEE ON EMBLEM

Alabama
- J.F. Gillem

Alaska
- James Hawley

Arizona
- Fred B. Townsend

Arkansas
- Wendell Robertson

California
- V.W. Gerhard

Colorado
- M.C. Dameron

Connecticut
- J.S. Hurley

Delaware
- E.H. Kane

District of Columbia.
- W.G. Glenn

Florida

- Mr. Bell

Georgia
- J.G. Juett

Hawaii
- J.P. Morgan

Idaho
- Paul Davis

Illinois
- W.C. Mundt

Indiana
- N.J. Buskirk

Iowa
- A.M. Pond

Kansas
- Foss Farar

Kentucky
- H. Reingold

Louisiana
- W.A. Coon

Maine
- Frank M. Hume

Maryland
- T.H. Scaffe

Massachusetts
- H.H. Wheelock

Michigan
- P.W. Nickel

Minnesota
- Conrad Veit

Mississippi
- W.T. Adams

Missouri
- U.P. Haw

Montana
- Worth C. Almon

Nebraska
- R.J. Webb

Nevada
- T.J.D. Salter

New Hampshire
- Walter J. Hogan

New Jersey
- J.M. Pancoast

New Mexico

- F.B. Humphrey

New York
- F.W. Baldwin

North Dakota
- Wm. Stern

Ohio
- E.L. King

Oklahoma
- P.A. Fox

Oregon
- R.D. Grant

Pennsylvania
- L.L. Felts

Rhode Island
- F.V. Thurber

South Dakota
- J.C. Denison

Tennessee
- W.R. Craig, Jr.

Texas
- S.P. Boom

Utah
- Charles Parsons

Vermont
- Joseph Fontain

Virginia
- W.R. Trotter

Washington
- Fred. J. Shaw

West Virginia
- Sam. Solins

Wisconsin
- L.J. Woodworth

Wyoming
World War Veterans
- Geo. E. Davis

American Army Association
- T.R. Smith

COMMITTEE ON NEXT MEETING PLACE

Alabama
- F.M. Ladd

Alaska
- James Hawley

Arizona
- Ed. M. LeBaron

Arkansas
- Wm. G. Edgar

California
- B.O. Shuman

Colorado
- T.H. Wiles

Connecticut
- W.D. Copp

Delaware
- Geo. L. Evans

District of Columbia
- Louis P. Clephane

Florida
- Mr. Bell

Georgia
- R.L. Wilson, Jr.

Hawaiian Islands
- J.P. Morgan

Idaho
- Frank Estabrook

Illinois
- Grover Sexton

Indiana
- J.B. Reynolds

Iowa
- B.R. Finch

Kansas
- Charles I. Martin

Kentucky
- Frank Bernhaim

Louisiana
- Clifford Stem

Maine
- James L. Boyle

Maryland
- A.C. Solomon

Massachusetts
- Marcus Maddern

Michigan
- Frank J. Tobin

Minnesota
- Loren B. Roberts

Mississippi
- J.S. Fleming

Missouri
- L.C. Lozier

Montana
- Arthur Barry

Nebraska
- Allan Tukey

Nevada
- E.L. Malsbary

New Hampshire
- H.L. Hereaux

New Jersey
- A.S. Westcott

New Mexico
- S.S. Caldwell

New York
- Fred Gallager

North Carolina

North Dakota
- Wm. Stern

Ohio
- Ralph Pearce

Oklahoma
- W.T. Butts

Oregon
- E.J. Eivers

Pennsylvania
- A.I. McRae

Rhode Island
- Walter Sharkey

South Dakota
- Wm. G. Buell

Tennessee
- G.C. Milligan

Texas
- L. Nicholson

Utah
- Fred. Jurgensen

Vermont
- J. Watson Webb

Virginia

- G.R. Poole

Washington
- Albert Johnston

West Virginia
- Joseph Jackson

Wisconsin
- C.H. Foster

Wyoming

- Benj. Gregg

World War Veterans
- F.H. Rein

American Army Association
- J.A. Bernard

ROSTER

Alabama
- Chenoweth, Beach Mead, Birmingham. U.S.N.
- Gaston, Cecil D., Birmingham. Med. Corps U.S.A. and A.E.F.
- Gillem, Jennings F., Birmingham. 320 M.G. Bn.
- Graves, Bibb, Montgomery. 117th F.A.
- Inzer, J.W., Mobile. 14th Inf.
- Jacobs, Leroy R., Birmingham. 38th Inf.
- Jordan, Wm.M., Birmingham. Evac. Hosp. No. 11.
- Ladd, Frank M., Jr., Mobile. U.S.N.
- Long, F.M., Jasper. 7th Inf. 9th M.G. Bn.
- Lussier, Richard F., Birmingham. M.I.D. Gen. Staff.
- Murphy, Matthew H., Birmingham, 117th F.A.
- Reiss, Norman J., Mobile. Q.M.C.
- Stoddard, B.S., Mobile. 49th Inf.
- Yates, Joseph A., Birmingham, 117th F.A.

Alaska
- Hawley, Edgar T., Boise, Idaho. U.S.A.

Arkansas
- Burrow, G.M., Little Rock. 18th Inf.
- Doherty, William, Jonesboro. 153d Inf.
- Edgar, Wm.G., El Dorado. 153d Inf.
- Hamilton, Scott D., Fayetteville. 346th Inf.
- Harris, Joe S., Monticello. 153d Inf.
- Harrison, J.J., Little Rock. Care Pugh Printing Company. Instructor Tr. Camp.
- Herschel, Ivie, Marion. 154th Inf.
- Hurt, Garland, Newport. 162d Inf.
- Jackson, Thomas A., Little Rock. 154th Inf.
- Kinsworthy, B.S., Little Rock. Off. Tr. Camps.
- Lloyd, T.H., Paragould. I.C.O.T.S.
- Mathis, Ross, Cotton Plant. 2d Inf.
- Penix, Wm. Roy, Jonesboro. Kelly Fld., Tex.
- Robertson, W.A., Ft. Smith. 13th Aero Squad.
- Smith, E. Ross, Little Rock. 141 M.G. Bn.

- Stafford, John L., Springdale. 106th Am. Train 3 1st Div.
- Taylor, R.P., Paragould. Aerial Ob. C.A.C.
- Tillman, Fred A., Fayetteville, 12th F.A.
- Wood, Roy W., Little Rock. Naval Aviation.

Arizona
- Baker, Alexander B., Phoenix. 28th F.A.
- Bernard, E.P., Tucson. 47th M.G. Bn.
- Cassidy, M.E., Bisbee. Ad. Gen. Dep.
- Greenway, John C., Warren. 101st Inf.
- Lebaron, Edwin M., Mesa. 801st P. Inf.
- Townsend, Frank B., Phoenix. F.A.C.O.T.S.

California
- Bohlen, E.E., San Francisco. 347th F.A.
- Dibblee, Benj.H., San Francisco. F.A.C.O.T.S.
- Gearhart, B.W., Fresno. 609th Aero Sq.
- Hammond, Leonard C., San Francisco, 91st Aero.
- Houghton, A.D., Los Angeles. Am. Serv. League.
- Kelly, E.J., Los Angeles. 64th U.S. Inf.
- Mathewson, H.G., Alameda. C.A.C.
- Palmer, C.E.G., Coalinga. Canadians.
- Shuman, Blair S., San Francisco. 363d Inf.
- Slow, Ashfield E., San Francisco. 347th F.A.
- Woolwine, Clare W., Los Angeles. 8th Inf. Gen. St.

Colorado
- Allen, Robt. G., Denver. 305th Inf.
- Dameron, M.C., Pueblo. Camp Med. Supp. Depot.
- David, Morton M., Denver. 20th Inf.
- Dickson, Ray, Ft. Collins. 30th Serv. Co.
- Gwin, Jno. W., Pueblo. 158th Inf.
- Krueger, Edw., Jr., Buena Vista. Air Serv.
- Lawrence, C.W., Pueblo. U.S.N.
- Maloney, B.F., Pueblo. 815th Pioneer.
- Myer, E.R., Boulder. 356th Inf.
- Saidy, H.A., Colorado Springs. 341st F.A.
- Sparr, D.J., Denver. 157th Inf.
- Stubbs, Albert L., La Junta. Medical Corps.
- Swink, Walter E., Rocky Ford. U.S.N.
- Wiles, Thos H., Denver. Chaplain.

Connecticut
- Butterworth, Dr. S., New Haven. Chem. War Serv.
- Calhoun, Philo C., Bridgeport. U.S.M.C.
- Carroll, Francis W., Waterbury. Presidential Gd. U.S.A.
- Copp, Webster D., Norwich, 301st M.G. Bn.
- Hurley, Jas. S., Waterbury. 73rd Inf.

- Malone, Wm. J., Bristol. A.S. (A).
- Matthies, Bernard H., Seymour. 105th Spruce Squad.
- Meservo, Harry C., Stamford. 68th C.A.C.
- Moody, Jas. B., Jr., Hartford. 301st Supply Train.
- Phillips, Alfred N., Jr., Stamford. 55th F.A.
- Sampsell, P.L., New London. U.S.N.
- Tiley, Morton C., Essex. U.S.A.A.S.

Delaware
- Doris, Geo. N., Wilmington. 364th Inf.
- Evans, Geo. L., Wilmington. U.S.N.
- Warner, Irving, Wilmington. Cement Mill Co. No. 8.

District of Columbia
- Clephane, Lewis P., Washington. U.S.N.
- Connolly, Frank A., Washington. 312th F.A.
- Fisk, Howard S., Washington. U.S.N.
- Glenn, Wm. G., Washington. 103d M.O.R.S.
- Hines, L.C., Washington. F.H. 165-117.
- Johnston, Chas. E., Washington. U.S. Coast Gd.
- Jones, E. Lester, Washington. Sig. Corps.
- Kruit, Prentiss, Washington. U.S.N.
- Leonard, H., Washington. U.S.M.C.
- Macgregor, Donald, Washington. Sig. Corps.
- Mulford, J.B., Washington. 165th Field Hosp. Co.
- Smith, Jno. L., Washington. Mil. Intell. Div.
- Turnage, M.C., Washington. P.M.G.O.

Florida
- Forster, Davis, New Smyrna. M.C.
- Givens, Morris M., Tampa. 31st Div.
- Lowry, S.L., Jr., Tampa. 31st Div.
- Mcgucken, Harold, Tampa. 124th Inf.
- Wigginton, J.T., Miami. 124th Inf.

Georgia
- Bell, Louis H., Atlanta. 20th M.G. Bn.
- Hillyer, Haywood H., Macon. 49 M.G. Bn.
- Juett, J.G., Atlanta. 122d. Inf.
- Siebert, Eugene, Atlanta. 437th Det. Eng. Corp.
- Stockbridge, Basil, Atlanta. 122d. Inf.
- Wilson, Robt. L., Jr., Atlanta. 122d Inf.

Hawaiian Islands
- Morgan, Jas. P., Hawaii. Inf. Replac. Troops Camp Grant, Ill.

Idaho
- Boom, Eugene C., Moscow. 18th Eng.
- Booth, C.M., Pocatello. 44th Inf.
- Collier, L.R., Pocatello. 163d Inf.

- Cummins, Taylor, Twin Falls. Coast Art.
- Davis, Paul, Boisé. I.C.O.T.S.
- Estabrook, Frank, Nampa. 146th M.G. Bn.
- Feeney, Thos. A., Lewiston.
- Green, Jno. S., Twin Falls, 1st St. Inf.
- Peterson, Paul T., Idaho Falls. 75th Inf.
- Wilson, Albert H., Clarks Fork. Q.M.C.
- Wilson, R.R., Pocatello. Inf. (unassigned).

Illinois
- Adams, M.E., Chicago. Q.M.C.
- Adler, Morris, Quincy. 1st O.T. Sch.
- Allen, Royal B., Marseilles. Q.M.C.
- Arnold, B.J., Chicago. Air Serv.
- Ayres, Lester G., Oak Park. C.A. School.
- Bolin, Jas. R., Paris. 2d Div.
- Boose, Jos. I., Chicago. U.S.N.R.F.
- Burnett, Geo., Shelbyville. 130th Inf.
- Burns, J.H., Carrollton. 337th F.A.
- Busch, A.H., Cicero. 117th M.G. Bn.
- Cave, Robt. R., Chicago. Q.M.C.
- Collins, W.H., Decatur. 119th Inf.
- Cummings, Jno. P., Chicago. Tank Corps.
- Currier, C.L., La Grange. 25th Eng.
- Dickerson, Earl B., Chicago. 365th Inf.
- Dutcher, Everett C., Dixon. 342d Inf.
- Eisenberg, Sam J., Chicago. 332d F.A.
- Engle, Robt. H., Freeport. 41st Inf.
- Everson, Chas. W., Chicago. A.S. Sig. R.C.
- Fayart, L.E., Springfield, 9th F.A.
- Field, Marshall, Chicago. F.A.
- Flannery, Frank B., Chicago, Beach Hotel, 221st F. Sig. Bn.
- Flory, Roger, Chicago. U.S.N.R.F.
- Floyd, Jno. A., Chicago. 6th Cav.
- Forman, Harold, Chicago. 72d F.A.
- Freid, Sam'l L., Chicago. 50th Inf.
- Goldberg, B.L., Chicago. U.S.N.R.F.
- Gorey, Thos. V., Joliet. Q.M.C.
- Gowenlock, Thos. R., Chicago. 1st Div.
- Greene, Jno. J., Chicago. C.M.G.O.T.S.
- Hana, Leo G., Peoria. 341st Inf.
- Hardwood, Thos. F., Bloomington. 343d Inf.
- Harrison, F.J., Streator. 1st C.O.T.S.
- Hartford, C.E., Marseilles. Ordnance.
- Hartrick, Guy R., Urbana. Ordnance.

- Helfrich, Geo. R., Chicago. 17th Inf.
- Hindert, Geo. C., Minonk. U.S.N.
- Hippler, S.H., Canton. 5th Reg.
- Hirstein, A.K., Fairbury. 129th Inf.
- Hughes, Jno. E., Chicago. A.S.
- Ickes, Fay, Springfield, 310th F. Sig. Bn.
- Jefferson, E.A., Chicago. 604th Eng.
- Jenkins, Newton, Chicago. 5th Reg.
- Kearney, Marshall V., Chicago. 303d Bn. Tank Corps.
- Kelley, W.L., Shelbyville. Chem. War Serv.
- Kendrick, J.E., Lincoln. 161st Dep. Br.
- Kingston, Ray, Shelbyville. 119th Inf.
- Kraatz, C.F., Carbondale. 161st D.B.
- Lauer, Robt. J., Chicago. 344th Inf.
- Lee, Harry V., Chicago. Signal Corps.
- Ling, Walter, Evansville. 115th Inf.
- Lynde, Cornelius, Chicago. U.S.N.R.F.
- Macaulay, Irwin, Quincy. Ordnance.
- Markley, H.G., Watseka. 116th Eng.
- Marsh, A.F., Chicago. Const. Div.
- Marshall, Thos. H., Chicago. Inf.
- McCauley, W.R., Olney. 308th Bn. Tank Corps.
- Meierhofer, Edw. H., Minonk. 68th Art.
- Merrick, Marlowe M., Chicago. Sig. Corps.
- Middleton, A.B., Pontiac. M.C., 90th Div.
- Miles, Grant M., Pontiac. 339th Inf.
- Miller, Jno. S., Jr., Winnetka. 33d F.A.
- Miller, Thos., Chicago. 49th Inf.
- Mock, Harry E., Chicago. Med. Corps.
- Mundt, Wm. C., Fairbury. Radio School.
- O'Connell, R.M., Bloomington. U.S.N.R.F.
- Oppenheimer, J., Chicago. 333d F.A.
- Orr, Ponce B., Joliet. 1st Inf.
- Packwood, Lawrence, Chicago. 521st M.T.C.
- Paddock, Geo. A., Evanston. 342d Inf.
- Parker, Howard K., Taylorville. 106th F.A.
- Pesavento, A.J., Joliet. R.S. and C.O.T.S.
- Pietrzak, Michael, Oglesby. A.S.A.P. 9th Dt.
- Powell, Wm. J., Chicago. 365th Inf.
- Reed, F.N., Evanston. 10th F.A.
- Reeder, Russel, Canton, 1st Co. C.A.C.
- Rhodes, Ben. S., Bloomington. 345th Inf.
- Rominger, W.E., Shelbyville. 14th M.G.
- Sayre, C.B., Canton. 326th F.A.

- Seaman, Geo. G., Taylorville. 17th F.A.
- Searcy, Earl B., Springfield. 311th Inf.
- Sedweak, C.E., Chicago. Q.M.C.
- Sexton, Grover F., Chicago. 108th Mil. Pol. Train.
- Simons, J.E., Glen Ellyn. U.S.M.C.
- Simpson, Sidney E., Carrollton. 164th Inf.
- Skubic, Edw. P., Chicago. C.O.T.S.
- Spencer, R.V., Chicago. 160th D.B.
- Sprague, A.A., Lake Forest. 341st Inf.
- Stello, Jno. H., McLeansboro. 115th M.G. Bn.
- Tapp, H.F., Quincy. U.S.N.R.F.
- Walsh, Martin, Chicago. 1st Repl. Reg.
- Webber, R.W., Urbana. 210th Aero Sq.
- Werckman, Jno. C., Minonk. 6th Repl. Reg.
- Werner, R.L., Peoria. U.S.N.R.F.
- Wham, Chas., Centralia. F.A.C.O.T.S.
- Young, R., Joliet. 41st Inf.
- Zerwekh, Paul W., Alton. Aviation.

Indiana

- Asch, A.L., Indianapolis. Q.M.C.
- Brewer, Scott R., Indianapolis. Air Serv.
- Buskirk, N.J., Bloomington. 111th Inf.
- Caster, Solon J., Indianapolis, 150th F.A.
- Clee, Robt. E., Kokimo. 69th F.A.
- Davis, Paul Y., Bloomfield. 335th Inf.
- Duddleston, A.C., Terre Haute, 151st Inf.
- Hogan, H.G., Ft. Wayne. M.T.C.
- Johnson, F.B., Indianapolis. Adv. Gen.
- Levi, Morris R., Evansville. 42d and 32d Div.
- Lonn, A.E., Laporte. 167th Brg.
- Mcdonald, T.M., Princeton. F.A. Repl. Tr.
- Moorhead, R.L., Indianapolis. 139th F.A.
- Newgent, L.R., Indianapolis. U.S.N.
- Putt, Geo., Indianapolis. Motor Trans. Corp.
- Reynolds, Jno. B., Indianapolis. Air Serv.
- Royer, S.D., Terre Haute. 349th Inf.
- Royze, Jno. A., Indianapolis. M.T.C.
- Strodel, C.F., Huntington. Inf.
- Thomas, Mark H., Huntington. Q.M.C.
- Timko, Jos. J., Brazil.
- Todd, Joe W., Hammond. Air Serv.
- Umpleby, Jay A., Gary. 139th F.A.
- Waltz, Ralph H., Noblesville. F.A.C.O.T.S.
- Watts, Albert H., E. Chicago, 139th F.A.

- Wilson, A.B., Indianapolis. 87th Div.
- Wolfe, C.P., Indianapolis. U.S.N.R.F.
- Ziisel, Frank F., Elkhart. 159th D. Br.

Iowa
- Berger, P.F., Carroll. 163d Disch. Off.
- Brookhart, S.W., Washington. Inf.
- Brookhart, T.L., Washington. M.T.C.
- Cole, J.F., Oelwein. 161st Depot Brig.
- Cook, Don C., Cedar Rapids. U.S.M.C.
- Circe, Wm. L., Bloomfield. 1st Eng.
- Cronin, Edw. P., Victor. U.S.N.
- Day, J.R., Council Bluffs, 19th Div.
- Dewolf, M.E., Spencer, 5th Inf.
- Doran, Lucien S., Beaver. 339th F.A.
- Finch, Budd R., West Union. 126th F.A.
- Hahn, F.K., Cedar Rapids. 126th F.A.
- Ham, Jos. P., Dubuque. 168th Inf.
- Harker, Frank C., Ottumwa. 168th Inf.
- Hart, W.R., Iowa City, 305th B. Tank Corp.
- Hudson, Fred M., Pocahontas. 79th A.A. Bn.
- Hungerford, Jno., Jr., Carroll. Air Serv.
- Kelly, J.H., Sioux City, 99th Inf.
- Kins, Will L., Hubbard. 159th Dept. Br.
- Lemley, H.D., Melrose. 109th Eng.
- Macvicar, Jno., Des Moines. Q.M.C.
- Malcomb, Earl, Laurens. 12th Inf.
- Metzger, T.M., Council Bluffs. 168th Inf.
- Neustrand, Oscar, Red Oak. U.S.N.R.F.
- Newell, Floyd, Ottumwa. M.C.
- Pattee, L.C., Pocahontas. Sig. Corp.
- Pease, Liberty, Farragut. 168th Inf.
- Plaister, R.M., Dubuque. 163d Inf.
- Polk, Harry H., Des Moines. 176th Inf.
- Pond, Alanson M., Dubuque. Med. Corps.
- Pusey, McGee, Council Bluffs. 11th Bal. Co.
- Schultz, E.R., Sioux City. Nav. Res. Fly. Corps.
- Shaw, Robt. J., Hayesville. 40th Inf.
- Smith, R.A., Council Bluffs. 163d D.B.
- Soper, B.M., Nevada. Q.M.C.
- Strotz, Roy R., Des Moines. 16th Inf.
- Thomas, Lee A., Mondamin. 3d Con. Bn.
- Welch, C.J., Denison. 4th Repl. Reg. 16th Co. C.O.T.S.

Kansas
- Barclay, Jas. F., Kansas City, 110th Eng.

- Bly, Wm. D., Leavenworth. 365th Inf.
- Branaman, H.A., Ottawa. 137th Inf.
- Brickell, J.B., Emporia. Med. Corps.
- Burnett, R.H., Dodge City. Zone Sup. Of. N.Y.C.
- Clausen, E.W., Atchison. U.S.N.A.S.
- Cubbison, P.K., Kansas City. 354th Inf.
- Eaton, L.R., Neodesha. 8th Eng.
- Elias, C.R., La Crosse. U.S.N.R.F.
- Farrar, Foss, Arkansas City. I.C.O.T.S.
- Foulston, S.L., Wichita, 91st Div.
- Grieves, Loren C., Ft. Leavenworth. G.S. Reg. A.
- Hantla, Jno. P., Spearville. 137th Inf.
- Hasty, Lewis A., Wichita. 342d Inf.
- Holden, Harley E., Neodesha. P.O. Dept.
- Holloway, W.W., Kansas City. P.M.G.O.
- Johnson, Paul R., Independence. U.S.N.
- Kurtz, W.P., Columbus. 158th D.B.
- Lambert, I.E., Emporia. Air Serv.
- Lee, Thos. A., Topeka. 26th Inf.
- Leekley, R.M., Arkansas City. 338th F.A.
- Madden, Jno., Sr., Wichita. Air Serv.
- Martin, Chas. I., Topeka. 70th Inf. Br.
- Metcalf, W.S., Lawrence. 77th Brig.
- Moss, Sidney A., Wichita. 125th F.A.
- Musselman, N.B., Arkansas City. R.M.A.
- O'Reilly, H.C., Strong City. 164th Depot Br.
- Ortmeyer, H.A., Wichita. 326th M.G. Bn.
- Pharen, W.A., Wichita. 360th Inf.
- Snyder, Harry E., Council Grove. Med. Det.
- Sparks, Keith L., Greensburg. Med. Dep.
- Stanford, F.C., Independence. A.S.S.C.
- Walker, H. Jos., La Crosse. 418th Eng.
- Weed, M.S., Lawrence. 137th Inf.
- Williams, Jno. W., Ottawa. Air Serv.
- Woods, Jas. A., Arkansas City. 101st Fld. Sig. B.
- Woodside, L.N., Council Grove. 13th Cav.

Kentucky
- Beard, B.F., Hardensburg. 138th F.A.
- Bell, Ulric J., Louisville. Inf.
- Bernheim, Fr. D., Louisville. 159th D.B.
- Bronaugh, Robt. L., Nicholasville. 164th Inf.
- Evans, Lynn B., Lebanon. U.S.N.R.F.
- Ewall, Geo. R., Louisville. 159th D.B.
- Fischer, A.T., Louisville. A.S.R.C.

- Fraser, V.C., Wickliffe. 6th Inf.
- Gordon, M.K., Madisonville. I.G.D.
- Hall, Herman H., Viper. 327th F.A.
- Hill, J. Murray, Bowling Green. U.S.N.R.F.
- Juett, J.G., Wickliffe. 18th Inf.
- Marriner, E.H., Dayton. 131st Inf.
- Moorman, H.D., Hardinsburg. 10th F.A.
- Muir, Edmund A., Nicholsville. 22d Ret. Co. G.S.
- Ringgold, J.H., Jr., Russellville. Air Sq. 260.
- Sachs, D.A., Jr., Louisville. U.S.N.R.F.
- Slack, R.H., Owensboro. 1st O.T.S.
- Sosnin, M.L., Louisville. Base Hosp. Camp Crane, Luxemberg, Fr.
- Soyars, Wm. O., Hopkinsville. U.S.M.C.
- Stewart, Phil. H., Paducah. M.R.C.
- Wheeler, Jas. G., Paducah. 159th D.B.
- Young, Jno. S., Glasgow. Med. Corps.

Louisiana
- Beard, L.P., New Orleans. U.S.N.R.F.
- Blancand, Gus, New Orleans. Co. 10.
- Coon, Wm. A., New Orleans. 73d F.A.
- Davis, Edw., New Orleans, 1st Reg. F.A.R.D.
- Ginella, Louis, New Orleans. M.C.
- Michel, F. Ralph, New Orleans. 46th F.A.
- Moore, Levering, New Orleans. Q.M.C.
- Owen, Allison, New Orleans. 141st F.A.
- Pratt, Geo. H.H., New Orleans. Air Serv.
- Stem, C.H., New Orleans. 2d Eng.
- Weinmann, R.J., New Orleans, 151st F.A.

Maine
- Adams, W.P., Portland. 54th Ar. C.A.C.
- Boyle, Jas. L., Augusta, 101st San. Tr.
- Greene, Roger A., Lewiston. 101st Trench Mort. Bn.
- Greenlaw, Albert, Eastport. Hdq. 26th Div.
- Haines, Roy C., Ellsworth. 334th Tank Corps.
- Humer, Frank M., Houlton. 103d U.S. Inf.
- Milliken, Carl E., Augusta.
- Norton, W.P., Portland. 72d Art. C.A.C.
- Presson, Geo. Mcg., Augusta. Adj. Gen.
- Robinson, A.L., Portland. 7th A.A. Bn.

Maryland
- French, Findlay H., Baltimore. S.O. Camp, Greenleaf, Ga.
- Good, Stuart S., Baltimore. 110th F.A.
- Huster, Wm. A., Cumberland. 113th Inf.
- Johnson, Willard J., Baltimore. 351st F.A.

- Knapp, Raleigh T., Baltimore, 110th F.A.
- Randall, A., Baltimore. 110th F.A.
- Scaffe, Harold, Baltimore. 14th F.A.
- Solomon, Adolph C., Baltimore. U.S.M.C.
- Stewart, Davis G., Baltimore. 351st F.A.
- Tieman, George H., Baltimore. Air Service.
- Wilmer, William B., Baltimore. Tank Corps.
- Young, Frank A., Cumberland, 115th Inf.
- Young, Harvey W., Baltimore. 351st F.A.

Massachusetts
- Bacon, G.G., Jamaica Plains. 316th F.A.
- Baldwin, H.L., Malden.
- Burt, C.E., New Bedford. 121st F.A.
- Cleary, Jas. P., Boston. Personnel Off. Camp Upton.
- Cutler, Geo. C., Jr., Boston. U.S.N.
- Dalton, Edward P., Boston. A.G.D.
- Dolan, W.H., Fitchburg. 26th Div.
- Foy, F.H., Quincy. 82d Div. Inf.
- Frothingham, L.A., N. Easton. Adj. Gen.
- Germain, Chas. F., Wollaston. 234th Eng.
- Gilbody, Geo. F., Boston.
- Green, Donald R., Holyoke. 28th F.A.
- Herbert, J.P.J., Worcester. 102d F.A.
- Howard, W.J., Whitman. 113th Eng.
- Jackson, L.P., Athol. 74th Inf.
- Madden, Marcus E., 64 N. Beacon St., 71 Art. C.A.C.
- Maniff, Harry, Revere. U.S.N.
- Marley, Thos. J., E. Boston. 104th Inf.
- McGrath, Jas. P., Roslindale. Hdq. 26th Div.
- McInnis, Victor A., Roxbury. 301st Inf.
- Moynihan, Neil P., Haverhill. C.O.T.S., Camp Lee, Va.
- Nolan, David J., Worcester. 52d Inf.
- O'Rourke, Jno. J., Lowell, 101st Sup. Tr.
- Page, Kenneth B., Longmeadow. 104th Inf.
- Peabody, J.C.R., Boston. Asst. to Dept. Insp., N.E. Dept. I.G. 5th Div. A.E.F.
- Pryor, J.H., West Newton 372d Inf.
- Rosenfeld, Jay C., Pittsfield. 359th Inf.
- Safford, Ralph K., Springfield. 104th Inf.
- Scott, H.J., Roxbury. 26th Div.
- Shinnick, Wm. T., Brockton. 55th Reg. C.A.C.
- Spillane, Leo A., Chelsea. Hdq. N.E. Dept.
- Stewart, H.J., Camp Devens. 36th Mis. Inf.
- Strandquist, H.W., Newton. 102d M.G.Bn.

- Thomas, H.C., Allston. 101st Eng.
- Wheelock, H.H., Fitchburg. 101st Sup. Tr.
- Williams, Harry R., Boston. 101st Am. Tr.

Michigan

- Alger, Frederick M., Detroit. 310th Amun. Tr.
- Allen, Carlos R., Detroit. 125th Inf.
- Baldwin, Paul R., Manistique. Air Service.
- Bellows, Benj. B., Highland Park. Ordnance.
- Bersey, John S., Lansing. Adjt. Gen., Michigan.
- Bowden, Isaac, Port Huron. Base Hosp. No. 73.
- Brink, Howard C., Grand Rapids. 126th Inf.
- Burgess, Frank, Grand Rapids. 126th Inf.
- Christie, J.T.C., U.S.A. Gen. Hop., No. 36, Detroit. Q.M.C.
- Conway, Bertram, 33 Cardoma St., Detroit. 367th Inf.
- Doyle, A.G., Grand Rapids. 126th Inf.
- English, Rand P., Detroit. 125th Inf.
- Evans, Lynn B., University Club, Detroit. U.S.N.R.F.
- Fehrenbocher, Chriss, 271 Harrison St., Gary, Ind. 10th Inf.
- Gildersleeve, Howard, Grand Rapids. U.S.N.R.F.
- Gilleo, Avery C., Grand Rapids. 126th Inf.
- Guelff, John J., Marquette. 328th F.A.
- Hall, William D., Kalamazoo. 126th Inf.
- Hansen, Myron J., Laurium. S.A.T.C.
- Harris, H.H., Detroit. A.S.S.C. Aviation Training.
- Henry, D.D., Grand Rapids. U.S.N.R.F.
- Hullfish, Henry G., Washington, D.C. Medical Dept.
- Kelley, Charles D., West Detroit. 32d Div.
- Kesl, G.M., Port Huron. M.D.
- Kilmer, Edward H., Grand Rapids. 10th Inf.
- King, William, Detroit. 125th Inf.
- Larson, Werner R., Ironwood. Sanitary Squad No. 58.
- Lawson, Otto Emil C.Y., Detroit. U.S.N.R.F.
- Lockhart, Arthur, Grand Rapids. U.S.N.R.F.
- Maines, George H., Battle Creek. 338th Inf.
- McKee, Mark T., Mt. Clemens. Chemical Warfare.
- McMahan, F.V., 322 E. Grand Blvd., Detroit. U.S.N.R.F.
- Moerisch, E.L., Escanaba. U.S.N.
- Nickel, P.W., Grand Rapids. U.S.N.R.F.
- Norton, Albert H., Detroit. 125th Inf.
- O'Brien, Thomas, Grand Rapids. U.S.N.
- O'Dell, H.A., Detroit. Hdg. Chief Engr.
- Quasigroch, Lee J., Highland Park, Ill., Camp Custer.
- Smith, George L., Detroit. 4th Tex. Inf.
- Tabor, Lyle D., Detroit. U.S.N.R.F.

- Tarpestra, George, Grand Rapids. 154th Aero Squad.
- Taylor, W.J., Port Huron. Hdq. Det. 14th Div.
- Tobin, Frank J., Jackson. 126th Inf.
- Veldmar, Edwin, Grand Rapids. 26th Inf.
- Weir, Orville H., Detroit. 125th Inf.
- Wilkin, H.H., Detroit. U.S.N.
- Young, Jay P., 706 Easterly Ave., 125th Inf.

Minnesota
- Ahern, Jno. J., St. Paul. 88th Inf.
- Anderson, S.E., Ruthton. 351st Inf.
- Baldwin, C.H., Redwood Falls. 87th Inf.
- Caldwell, Jno. C., Albert Lea. 127th F.A.
- Chapin, Geo. S., St. Paul. 167th Inf.
- Clark, Gordon M., Duluth. 125th F.A.
- Clipper, Geo. A., St. Paul. Q.M.C.
- Cook, Paul B., Lowrny Blg., St. Paul. Med. Corp.
- Eaton, M.E., Minneapolis. 309th Fld. Sig. Bn.
- Fowler, F.J., St. Paul. Camp McArthur.
- Fuller, Harrison, St. Paul. 163d F.A.
- Hall, Levi M., Minneapolis. 124th F.A.
- Henderson, R.L., Minneapolis. C.A.
- King, S.W., Austin. Motor Mechanic.
- Lewis, H.B., Minneapolis. Dunwoody Tr. Det.
- Lowther, Geo., Minneapolis. Sig. Corp.
- Macmichael, P.R., 119 N. 4th St., Minneapolis. I.C.O.T.S.
- Magnusson, C.W., Hibbing. 85th F.A.
- McCarthy, E.D., St. Paul. 313th Eng.
- Nelson, A.M., Fairmont. 68th Inf. Br.
- Nelson, Roy, Minneapolis. M.G.S.
- Nolan, M.C., Grand Meadow. Q.M.C.
- Page, Ralph W., Minneapolis. 303d Cav.
- Parks, Jno. J., St. Paul. 101 Aero Squad.
- Partridge, C.A., Owatonna. 332d M.G. Bn.
- Roberts, Loren B., Little Falls. 187 Aero Sq., A.E.F.
- Rogers, M.J., St. Paul. 74th Eng.
- Schaub, H.W., St. Paul. 65th Pioneer Inf.
- Smith, S.S., Worthington. 164th D. Brig.
- Stromgren, E., Center City. Motor Amb. Sup. Dep. Louisville.
- Sturtz, Wm. P., Albert Lea. U.S.N.R.F.
- Tomelty, Jas. C., Little Falls. 337th F.A.
- Ustruck, W.J., Montevideo. 346th Inf.
- Vancma, Geo., Lakefield. 151st Aero Sq.
- Varner, C.L., St. Cloud. Naval Aviation.
- Veit, Con., 3733 Pleasant Ave., Minneapolis. 70th Inf.

- Warner, Lee F., St. Paul. Chem. Warfare.
- Williams, W.A., 621 Byron St., Mankato. 2d Eng.

Mississippi
- Adams, Wm. T., Jr., Corinth, 115th F.A.
- Alexander, Jno. M., Jackson. San. Corp.
- Burnett, Robt., Vicksburg. 334th M.G. Bn.
- Chambers, Paul, Jackson. U.S.N.R.F.
- Clark, Arthur B., Indianola. 79th Div.
- Dalbey, Chas. R., Jackson, 115th Inf.
- Dunn, Arthur Jno., Vicksburg. 162d Inf.
- Fitzhugh, Alex., 1403 Baum St., Vicksburg. Comp Q.M., Camp Hancock, Ga.
- Fleming, Jas. S., Jr., Natchez. 52d Ammun. Tr.
- Hoskins, Geo. C., Brookhaven. 162d Inf.
- Sullens, Frederick, Jackson. Mil. Intell. Div. Gen. Staff.
- Whiting, Jno. S., Jr., Farrell. 24th Co. C.O.T.S.

Missouri
- Albert, Wilfred G., St. Louis. 57th F.A.
- Alexander, F., St. Louis. 49th Inf.
- Allen, C.P., Trenton. Field Ord.
- Barco, A.U., St. Louis. U.S.N.R.F.
- Bennett, J.M., Neosho. S.M.A.
- Bernard, J.A., St. Louis. 45th U.S. Inf. Medical Corps.
- Bradbury, H.C., Jefferson City. U.S.M.C.
- Bruggere, W.H., St. Louis. 342d F.A.
- Cambell, C.W., Sedalia. 314th Eng.
- Carter, A., Meadville. 18th Inf.
- Clark, Bennett, Bowling Green. 88th Div.
- Clarke, Harvey C., Jefferson City. 35th Div.
- Cronkite, D.W., St. Joseph. Naval Aviation.
- Dallmeyer, Phil. A., Jefferson City. I.C.O.T.S.
- Daly, Richard L., St. Louis. 12th F.A.
- Dickson, J.T., Warrensburg. U.S.N.R.F.
- Dimmitt, C.P., St. Louis. Hosp. Guard.
- Egger, E.R., St. Louis. 6th Reg. F.A.R.D.
- Field, Andrew, Macon. 160th D.B.
- Foster, Dick B., Kansas City. 10th Div.
- Fullerton, Rob., Louis, 111. 5th Mo. Inf.
- Garrett, Ruby D., Kansas City. Signal Corps.
- Good, H.G., Carthage. 116th Engrs.
- Gray, L.H., Carthage. 6th M.G.B. Marines.
- Green, Fredk. Wm., St. Louis. 12th Engrs.
- Grimsley, Clyde I., Salina. 16th Inf.
- Hagner, A.R., Hagerstown. Casual Air Serv.

- Haw, U.P., Benton. 90th Inf.
- Holcomb, H.W., Moberly. Q.M.C.S.C.
- Hubbard, Douglas, G., Versailles. 346th Inf.
- Huston, G.C., Troy. U.S.N.
- Hyde, L.M., Princeton. 338th Inf.
- Johnston, Gale, Mexico. U.S.N.R.F.
- Johnston, W.O., St. Louis. Bat. No. 60 Arty. C.A.C.
- Kealy, Philip J., Kansas City. 138th Inf.
- Klemm, K.D., Kansas City. 106th F.A.
- Krechel, Henry, Floissant. 128th F.A.
- Lafayette, D. Lytle, St. Louis. 332d Inf.
- Layton, Chas. O., St. Louis. Naval Veteran Assn.
- Leach, Merton H., Jefferson Barracks. Q.M.C.
- Lonergan, Wm. J., St. Louis. 138th Inf.
- Lozier, Lue C., Carrollton. 164th D.B.
- McKinley, C.A., Clinton. 60th Pioneer Inf.
- Monovill, Harold P., St. Louis. Naval Overseas Trans. Serv.
- Montgomery, P.S., St. Louis. 312th Inf.
- Nee, Dan M., Springfield. O.T.S.
- Neville, J.H., Springfield. 41st Arty.
- Raupp, William, Pierce City. 2d Pioneer Inf.
- Razoosky, Julius, St. Louis. Aero. Phot.
- Robinette, P.J., Hartville. U.S.M.C.
- Rogers, George, Missouri Ath. Assn. A.S. 133d Det.
- Rosemann, Henry, St. Louis. Tank Corps.
- Royal, Thomas V., St. Louis.
- Schields, Geo., St. Louis. Adj. Gen. Dept.
- Tucker, Paul, Lamar. 112th Inf.
- Wanchtes, Geo., St. Louis.
- Watkins, Charles, St. Louis. Fort Sheridan.
- Wheless, Joseph, St. Louis. Judge Adv.
- White, J.M., St. Louis. Eng.
- Woods, Joe, St. Louis. 354th Inf.
- Yount, M.P., Ironton. 3d O.T.L.

Montana
- Almon, Worth C., Helena. U.S.N.R.F.
- Barnett, Ben W., Helena. 163d D.B.
- Barry, Arthur N., Billings. A.S. Dept.
- Blomquist, H.L., Great Falls.
- McCallum, D.S., Helena. 163d Inf.
- Pew, Chas. E., Helena. 44th Inf.
- Sheridan, Chas. L., Bozeman. 49th Inf.

Nebraska
- Coad, Ralph G., Omaha. A.S.M.A.

- Fischer, Frank P., Scotts Bluff. 164th D.B.
- Fitzsimmons, L.L., Fremont. M.O.T.C.
- Gilligan, Geo W., Lincoln. 41st Inf.
- Goodrich, E.S., Fairbury. 305th Tank Corps.
- Holdeman, Geo. H., York. 125th F.A.
- Howard, Bert, Tecumseh. U.S.N.
- Kearney, Orlando H., Morrill. 13th Inf.
- McDermott, Ed. P., Kearney. C.M.G.O.T.S.
- McGuire, L.J., Omaha. 3d Inf.
- Madden, Ray J., Omaha, U.S.N.
- Maher, John G., Lincoln. Chief Disb. Officer, Paris.
- Mersinger, Leon, Plattsmouth. 222d Field Signal Bn.
- Rademacher, R.A., York. Unassigned.
- Ritchie, Wm., Jr., Omaha. 69th Inf.
- Robertson, Hugh C., Omaha. 356 San. Det.
- Stirch, J.A., Lincoln, 350th Inf.
- Stryker, Hird, Omaha. 338th F.A.
- Stuart, A.L., Fremont. 428 Eng., 109 Eng.
- Tukey, Allan A., Omaha. 26th Inf.
- Vanness, Clarence, Stanton. A.S.S.C.
- Webb, Robert J., Omaha. 164th Depot Brig.

Nevada
- Malsbary, E.L., Reno. 218th Eng.
- Salter, J.D., Winnemucca. 2d Co., 3d Bn. I.C.O.T.S.

New Hampshire
- Abbott, F.J., Manchester. 103d F.A.
- Deschems, Homar J., East Jaffey. Motor Supply Train.
- Fiske, George V., Manchester. 75th Div. San. Tr.
- Heureux, L'Herve, Manchester. 103d Inf.
- Hogan, Walter J., Manchester. 103d Inf.
- Knox, Frank, Manchester. 303d Amm. Tr.
- Maher, Charles F., 612 Main St., Laconia.
- Mahoney, Matthew J., Manchester. 103d Inf.
- Murphy, Wm., 49 Alfred St., 103d Inf.
- Santor, John, Manchester. 104th F.H.
- Sullivan, Wm. E., Nashua, 102d Inf.
- Trufant, Arthur, Hudson. 103d Inf.

New Jersey
- Besson, Harlan, Hoboken. 5th A.C.
- Brady, Charles S., Weehawken. 322d Sanitary Train.
- Bromley, Herbert L., 127 Clinton Ave., Clifton. Camp Hdq., Camp Dix.
- Cangemi, Angelo, Newark. U.S. Nitrate Plant, No. 1.
- Debevoise, Paul, Elizabeth. 312th Inf.

- Eggers, Alan L., Summit. 107th Inf.
- Ehrhardt, Philip, Jersey City, 111th M.G. Bn.
- McGrath, Edward A., Elizabeth. U.S.N.
- Mullik, D.B., Leonia. Eng. M.P.
- Pancoast, John M., Hancock's Bridge. U.S.N.R.F.
- Ritter, Ralph F., Rahway. Staff, Ft. Hancock.
- Schenck, R.P., Jersey City. Q.M.C.
- Stratton, Gervas, Vineland. U.S.N.R.F.
- Tischbeck, John D., Newark. 112th H.F.A.
- Tobin, Ed. A., 27 Broadway, Camden. U.S.N.
- Weed, Newell P., 65 Union, Montclair. 344th Ban. Tank Corps.
- Wescoat, Absalom S., Atlantic City. M.C.

New Mexico
- Baca, Herman G., Belen. U.S.N.
- Baca, Jesus M., Santa Fe. 115th Pv. Hq.
- Blevins, Donald L., Las Vegas. 82d F.A.
- Cutting, B.M., Santa Fe. Mil. Attaché, London.
- Dillard, H. Wyatt, Roswell. 358th Inf.
- Doldwell, C.S., Albuquerque. Inf. (?)
- Flamm, Roy H., Alamogorda. 18th Eng. R.T.C. French Army.
- Humphreys, Fred. B., Dayton. U.S.N.

New York
- Allen, Freeman C., Rochester. Q.M.C.
- Baldwin, Frederic W., Brooklyn. 308th Inf.
- Ball, Grosvenor Lowrey, Lawrence. 306th Inf.
- Barnhill, George B., New York. 820th Aero Squad.
- Barrett, Walter N., Saratoga Springs. U.S.M.C.
- Baruck, S.L., New York. Q.M.C.
- Beers, W.H., New York. 601st Eng.
- Berry, Charles W., Brooklyn. 106th Inf.
- Black, John, Brooklyn. Stars and Stripes Gen. Staff.
- Bodamer, Harold L., Buffalo. U.S.N.R.F.
- Boeckel, Fred. W., Buffalo. 106th F.A.
- Booth, Robert C., Plattsburg. 303d Inf.
- Boyce, A.L., New York. Q.M.C.
- Bradley, Goodyear, Buffalo. 106th Regt.
- Bunn, Earle D., Newburgh. Train, and Unassign. Duty.
- Burrill, Louis D., Syracuse. U.S.N.R.F.
- Butler, William E., Brooklyn. Ambulance Service.
- Church, Elihu C., New York. 117th Eng.
- Compton, Geo. B., New York. 153d Depot Bri. F.A.
- Conway, Thomas J., Ithaca. U.S. Marines.
- Cooke, James P., New York. 106th Inf.
- Cosby, Arthur P., New York. A.G.O.

- Daggett, Geo. F., Brooklyn. Military Intell. Div.
- Davies, Julien L., New York. U.S.N.R.F.
- Dean, Clark M., New York. 107th Inf.
- Declucq, Floyd L., Cortland. 108th Inf.
- Decoursey, Fales, New York. U.S.N.R.F.
- Derby, Richard, New York. 2d Div.
- Deyo, Harrison, Yonkers. S.A.T.C. Columbia Univ.
- Draper, Wm. H., New York. Co. 2, N.Y. Reg.
- Duell, Charles H., New York. U.S.N.
- Eckert, J.A., New York. 105th F.A.
- Engel, Nicholas, New York. 107th Inf.
- Finelite, A.C., New York. Q.M.C.
- Fish, Hamilton, Jr., New York. 369th Inf.
- Floyd, Chas. H., New York. 107th Inf.
- Fox, E.E., 58 W. 47th St., New York.
- Frank, Eugene, New York. E.O.T.S.
- Gallagher, F.T.C., Oswego. 108th Inf.
- Goerke, James P., Brooklyn. U.S.N.
- Hayes, Wade H., New York. 27th Div.
- Healy, Jos. P., New York. U.S.N.
- Helwig, A.L., 517 New York Eng. Corp.
- Hudson, Donald, New York. 27th Aero Squadron.
- Hunt, Clyde R., Woodhaven. 7th Bt. Hdqrs.
- Ingram, Lee, Gloversville. 105th Inf.
- Jay, Delancey K., Westbury. 307th Inf.
- Jennings, Allen D., Brooklyn. U.S.N.R.F.
- Kincaid, J. Leslie, Syracuse. 27th Div.
- Kitchel, Lloyd, Bronxville. 12th F.A.
- Knob, Frederick J., New York. U.S.M.C.
- Krumm, Edward Delos, Rome. 10th Inf.
- Lyons, William M., Brooklyn. 114th Inf.
- McAdoo, William Gibbs, Jr., New York. U.S.N. Air Service.
- McAlpin, Milo F., New York. 37th Art.
- McIlvaine, Tompkins, New York. Intell. Service.
- McKlaine, Osceala E., New York. 367th Inf.
- Marsh, Robert M.C., New York. 351st F.A.
- Mela, Harry F., New York. 152d Depot Bdg.
- Miller, Lawrence, New York, 305th F.A.
- Mosle, C. Fred., New York. 33d Inf.
- Mullin, R. Jerome, Brooklyn. 308th Inf.
- Munske, Charles R., Brooklyn. 102d F.A.
- Nickerson, Hoffman, New York. Ordnance.
- Okerlind, Melin A., Jamestown. U.S.N.T.S.
- Osborne, Fairfield, New York. 351st F.A.

- Perry, Francis W., Brooklyn. 77th Div.
- Press, Thomas C., Bronx. 105th F.A.
- Putnam, G.P., New York. F.A.C.O.T.S.
- Rackoff, Irwin Ira, New York. 152d Depot Brigade.
- Reid, D. Lincoln, New York. 369th Inf.
- Ridder, Joseph E., New York. M.T.C.
- Riffe, James, Elmira. 108th Inf.
- Robinson, Fordham Road and Valentine Ave., New York. General Staff.
- Robinson, Francis H., New York. Q.M.C.
- Roosevelt, Theodore, New York. 20th Inf.
- Schmidt, W.M., Pleasantville. 7th Inf.
- Seligman, J.L., New York. 27th Div.
- Smith, Powers C., Watertown. 307th F.A.
- Smith, Thomas R., St. Louis. A.S.D.
- Stone, Laue K., New York. 34th Aero Squadron.
- Swift, Parton, Buffalo, 151st F.A. Bri.
- Taylor, H. Irv., New York. C.A.C.
- Townson, K.C., Rochester. F.A.C.O.T.S.
- Van Buren, J.N., Dunkirk. Aviation.
- Wells, John, New York. 105th U.S. Inf.
- Wheat, Geo. S., New York. U.S.N.
- Wickersham, C.W., New York. 27th Div.
- Wiseman, Mark H., New York. 7th Regt.
- Wood, Eric P., New York. 83d Div.
- Wright, W.T., New York. 105th F.A.

North Dakota
- Baker, Julius R., Fargo. 6th Corps M.P. Co.
- Fraser, G.A., Bismarck. Inf. P.M.G.O.
- Gorman, Arthur, Fargo. 26th Inf.
- Hanley, J.M., Mandan. 148th M.G. Bn.
- Merry, Lyall B., W. Dickinson. 116th Supply Train.
- Semling, H.V., Bismarck. 116th Tr. Hdqrs.
- Stern, William, Fargo. Q.M.C.
- Treacy, Robt. H., Bismarck. 339th Inf. 160th Depot Brigade.
- Williams, J.P., No. Fargo. 3d Eng.

Ohio
- Babcock, Vearne C., Elyria. U.S. Naval Aviation.
- Bettman, Gilbert, 1114 Union Trust Bldg., Military Intell. Div.
- Bimm, Harry L., Dayton. Air Service.
- Black, Robert L., Cincinnati. 37th Div. Military Intell.
- Bruml, Maurice W., Cleveland. Air Serv.
- Bush, H.M., Briggsdale. 134th F.A.
- Campbell, L.J., Youngstown. 309th F.A.

- Cobe, Ralph D., Findlay. 145th Inf.
- Conklin, Wm. H., Columbus. Q.M.C.
- Fess, Thomas L., Yellow Springs. 394th M.G. Bri.
- Funm, Norbert E., Sandusky. 147th Inf.
- Gerlack, F.C., Wooster. 146th Inf.
- Hall, Joseph L., Cincinnati, 5th Corps Artillery.
- Hard, Dudley J., Cleveland. 135th F.A.
- Horrell, Olney W., Dayton. 134th F.A.
- Huston, C.H., Mansfield, 112th Am. Train.
- King, E.L., Dayton. Air Service.
- Kline, John H., Dayton. 62d F.A.
- Koons, Jack F., Cincinnati. 148th Inf.
- Lea, Andrew B., Cleveland. 112th Engrs.
- Macdougal, Harry O., Akron. Ordn.
- Mcgill, Don. R., Nelsonville. 308th Tr. M. Btry.
- Murray, Chas. J., Elyria. 42d Div.
- Nicklett, A.P., Toledo. U.S.N.R.F.
- Perry, George W., Youngstown. 1st Army, A.E.F.
- Phillips, Thomas A., Dayton. 812th Pio. Inf.
- Priddy, John E., Findlay. F.A.C.O.T.S.
- Ramsey, Andrew M., Cincinnati. 26th Div.
- Segal, Ben M., Cleveland. 135th F.A.
- Sonsley, Harry J., Ada. 62d F.A.
- Turner, Cyril B., Columbus. 308th T.M. Btry.
- Wilson, Chalmers, R., Columbus, 112th Field Sig. Bn.

Oklahoma
- Adkins, E.S., Muskogee. Hdq. 42d Div.
- Berry, Ralph H., Tulsa. 173d Inf.
- Burling, Wm. T., Sapulpa. I.C.O.T.S.
- Butts, R.B., Muskogee. 162d D.B.
- Chase, Val D., Alva. U.S.N.
- Fischer, F.W., Oklahoma City. Q.M.C.
- Fox, Philip A., Tulsa. 23d Engrs.
- Gingerich, H.A., Okmulgee. 358th Inf.
- Haugherty, Hugh, Enid. E.J.B.T.S.
- Hagan, Horace H., Tulsa. C.A.C.
- Hoffman, Roy, Oklahoma City. 93d Div.
- Keenan, Rob. B., Sapulpa. 308th Aero Squad.
- McNally, Earl, Okemah. 111th Amm. Train.
- Meyer, Howard W., U.S.S. Bank Bldg., U.S. Slipping Bd.
- Niles, Alva J., Tulsa. 7th Div.
- Norwood, Frank H., Prague. Ft. Riley.
- Sams, Vernett E., Wewoka. 49th Inf.
- Shea, Thomas J., Buffalo, N.Y. 56th F.A.

- Taylor, Max A., Pryor. 330th Inf.
- Thompson, N.A., 111 E. Latimer St., Tulsa. 57th Inf.
- Tully, B.L., 83d F.A.
- Viuer, Wm., Tulsa. S.O.T.S.

Oregon

- Critchlow, Harry, Portland. 363d Arab. Co.
- Eivers, Edw. J., Portland. 162d Inf.
- Follett, Will. B., Eugene. 69th F.A.
- Grant, Roderick D., Portland. Air Service.
- Leonard, Barge E., Portland. 63d Inf.
- May, John L., North Portland. 162d Inf.
- Mullen, C.L., Portland. U.S. Marines.
- Pargon, Joseph A., Portland. M.C.

Pennsylvania

- Aurand, Ammon M., Jr., Beaver Springs. Q.M.C.
- Beaman, Joseph W., Towanda. 140th Tank Corps.
- Becker, H.M., Pittsburgh. (?)
- Biddle, Charles J., Philadelphia. Air Serv.
- Blank, Harry C., Allentown. C.O.T.S.
- Bodin, F.S., Wellsboro. B.E.F.
- Buck, Howard, Philadelphia. 96 Aero Sq.
- Buettner, C.A., Johnstown. Amb. Co.
- Collins, J., East Pittsburgh. 371 Inf.
- Davis, Shanley, Pottsville. Aviation.
- Dearlove, Chas., Philadelphia. 109th Inf.
- Detrich, A., Philadelphia. School for A.R. & M.O.
- Dixon, F.E., Elkins Park. 318th F.A.
- Dobson, W.F., 284 N. Main St., Wilkes-Barre. U.S.N.R.F.
- D'Olier, Franklin, Philadelphia. Q.M.C.
- Dunkle, Ray, Dry Runn. 4th D.B.
- Dunn, Stewart, Pittsburgh. 83d F.A.
- Egloff, John, East Pittsburgh. 8th Trench Mort. Bat.
- Fischer, Andrew, Johnstown. 7th Eng.
- Flood, Frank, Pittsburgh. Chem. War. Service.
- Forester, I.G., Philadelphia. 46th Inf.
- Foster, David, Carnegie, 305th Field Sig. Bn.
- Geary, John W., Philadelphia. M.I.D.
- Gentzel, Paul, Bellefonte. 314th Inf.
- Greer, John, New York City. Nat. Cath. War Council.
- Hauth, M.L., Meadville. 29th Eng.
- Hecht, Carl C., c/o West Branch Knitting Co., U.S.M.C.
- Herbine, A.P., Berwick. 314th Inf.
- Hill, Frederick, Pittsburgh, 90th Inf.
- Hoeger, Adelbert, 1508 Sheffield St., Pittsburgh. 209th Eng.

- Hoopes, E.S., East End Ave., Beaver. Casual Air Service.
- Hosack, George, 1415 Park Blg., Pittsburgh, 111th Inf.
- Houck, Byron, Williamsport. 1st Reg. M.T.S.
- Hudoe, M.J., Uniontown. 306th Tank Corp.
- Hulings, Norman, Oil City. 22d Aero Sq.
- Hunsicker, Stanley, Collegeville. Q.M.C.
- Ivony, Leo, East Pittsburgh. I.C.O.T.S.
- Johns, Alexander, Monessen. 2d Eng. Tran. Regiment.
- Johnson, J.E., West Chester. 301st Tank Train.
- Johnson, Miller A., Lewisburg. 162d Inf.
- Jones, Warrel, Clearfield. 38th Inf.
- Katz, Edward, Honesdale. M.T.C.
- Keller, Oliver, Lancaster. Air Service.
- Knox, Andrew, Philadelphia. Med. Corps.
- Kresales, Kenneth, Easton. U.S.A.A.S.
- Krumbhaar, Edward, Chestnut Hill. Base Hos. No. 10.
- Lamond, James, Philadelphia. Avia. A.S.A.
- Laughlin, Alex., Jr., Sewickley. 88th Div.
- McCall, Joseph, Merion. 311th. F.A.
- McRae, A.K., Pittsburgh. M.T.C.T.S.
- Metz, Benj., Pittsburgh. 124th Eng.
- Morganroth, C.K., Shamokin. 312th Inf.
- Muench, William, Jr., Philadelphia. 606th Eng.
- Newcomer, Robert, Pittsburgh. 76th Div.
- Nofer, Geo., 621 Belgrade St. 3d Div. Hdq.
- O'Donnel, James, Philadelphia. 315th Inf.
- Pearson, Alfred, Jr., Somerset. 6th E.T.R.
- Pennel, Edred J., Norristown. 304th Ammun. Tr.
- Penny, Jos. M., Philadelphia. U.S.N.
- Phelps, L.M., Erie. 112th Inf.
- Putlk, Lawhend, Clearfield. Base Hosp. No. 4.
- Reasa, Thomas, Pottsville. 103d Eng.
- Rehr, Thomas, Pottsville. 103d Eng. Co. C.
- Reifsender, Russell, Pottstown. 182d Aero Sq.
- Rick, Geo., Reading. 302 Guard and Fire Co.
- Rigby, Howard, Pittsburgh. O.T.C.
- Samsel, Hugh, Stroudsburg. U.S.N.
- Saxe, Michael, Philadelphia. 54th Inf.
- Sembower, Guy, Reading, 114th Ord. Co.
- Shoeffer, Clinton, Pottsville. 103d Eng.
- Simonson, E.G., Philadelphia. 490 Aero Sq.
- Singer, Robert, Stroudsburg. 109th Inf.
- Smyth, William, Philadelphia. Engrs. Adj. Gen. Dept.
- Spangel, Lyell, Williamsport. U.S.N.

- Stevenson, Richard, Chester. Handley Page Training Dept.
- Tyler, George, Philadelphia, 311th F.A.
- Walsh, Joseph, Pittsburgh. 4th Eng.
- Wear, Byron, Hazleton. 146th Inf.

Philippine Islands
- Landon, Robert R., Manila. 111th Corps and 2d Army.

Rhode Island
- Angell, Carl H., Providence. F.A.C.O.T.S.
- Cantwell, Percey, Providence. 351st P.A.
- Eleoniskey, James, Main Crompton. Sig. Corps.
- Johnston, Alexander, Providence. C.A.C.
- McKannah, F., River Pt. Medical Corps.
- San Soneitr, Jos., 4 Claremont Ave., 103d F.A.
- Sharkey, Walter, Woonsocket. 151st D.B.
- Shunney, Wm. P., Woonsocket. 103d P.A.
- Sturges, Rush, Providence. Ord.
- Thurber, Fred B., c/o Tilden Thurber Co. U.S.N.
- Weeder, R.B., Providence. 103d F.A.

South Carolina
- Fulton, Robert, Florence. 105th Supply Tr.
- Lachicotte, N.S., Florence. U.S.N.R.F.
- Reed, Charles, Charleston. 365th Inf.
- Smyser, John, Florence. Med. Corps.

South Dakota
- Buell, William, Rapid City. 335th Inf.
- Dennison, John, Vermillion. C.M.G.O.T.S.
- Doud, F.R., Mobridge. 13th Eng.
- Johnson, T.R., Sioux Falls. 102d F.A.
- Maloney, Paul, Aberdeen. 163d F.A.
- Pfeiffer, Joseph, Rapid City. Ord.

Tennessee
- Anderson, Glenn, Nashville. C.A.C.
- Berry, Harry, Hendersonville. 115th F.A.
- Bolling, W.E., Nashville. 114th F.A.
- Bowman, Chas., Nashville. 2d Div.
- Brown, Barton, Nashville. 114th F.A.
- Buckner, Ed., Thompson's Station. 114th F.A.
- Buford, Ned, Nashville. Air Ser.
- Cason, Wm., Nashville. 114th F.A.
- Corson, Herbert, Nashville. U.S.N.
- Gleason, James, Knoxville. 114th F.A.
- Griffen, Eugene, Nashville, 114th F.A.
- Hager, Richard, Nashville, 115th F.A.
- Handler, Walter C., Memphis. 55th P.A. Brig.

- Hayes, John, Memphis. 114th F.A.
- Kleine, Kenneth E., Memphis. Unassigned.
- Lason, William, Nashville, 114th F.A.
- Lea, Luke, Nashville. 114th F.A.
- Mernt, Henry, Jacksonville, 115th F.A.
- Milligan, G.C., Chattanooga. 156th Dept. Brig.
- Milliken, Chattanooga. 81st Div.
- Naive, W.W., Clarkville. U.S.N.
- Oxe, Howard, Nashville, 114th F.A.
- Palmer, Ed., Nashville. 117th F.A.
- Robertson, John, Lebanon, 115th F.A.
- Shadow, W.A., Winchester. Air Ser.
- Spence, Carey, Knoxville. 117th Inf.
- Warning, Rome, Memphis. 33d Div.
- Watson, Lawrence, Columbia. 114th F.A.
- Winfry, Douglas, Memphis.

Texas

- Allen, Arch C., Dallas. 132d F.A.
- Bacon, Benjamin, Wichita Falls. 360th Inf.
- Beagley, John, La Porte. Inf.
- Beavens, C., Houston. 357th Inf.
- Birkhead, Claude, San Antonio, 131st F.A.
- Boon, S.P., Brady, 111th Sup. Train.
- Bradley, Rolland, Houston. 132d F.A.
- Carrel, Alfred, Austin. Air Ser.
- Cohn, E.M., Dallas. U.S.M.C.
- Foy, Hugh, Dallas. Army Tran. Service.
- Gaines, J.P., Bay City. 26th Inf.
- Grubbs, Roscoe, Paris, 5th M.G. Bn.
- Hoover, John, Houston. 143d Inf.
- Jackson, W.E., Hillboro. 141st Inf.
- Johnson, W.W., Galveston. U.S.N.
- King, John L., Ft. Worth, 111th Am. Train.
- Langdon, Russell, Houston. U.S.N.
- Lindsley, Henry, Dallas. Gen. Staff.
- Nicholson, Le Roy, Ballinger. U.S.N.
- Smith, C., Galveston. Inf.
- Tips, Chas., Three Rivers, 90th Div. Inf.
- Vameson, Rou A., Marlin. 143d Inf.
- Young, John, Austin. C.A.C.

Utah

- Douglas, Royal, Ogden. 81st Inf.
- Jurgensen, Fred, Salt Lake City. Gen.
- Kundson, J.C., Brigham City. 326th Inf.

- McCarty, Ray, Salt Lake City. U.S.N.
- Meehan, Leo, Salt Lake City. U.S.N.F.C.
- Parsons, C., Salt Lake City. Sant. Corps.
- Rhivers, Donald, Ogden. 18th Eng.
- Robertson, Baldwin, Salt Lake City. 362d Inf.
- Seely, L.J., Mt. Pleasant. 814th Aero Sq.
- Smoot, H.R., Salt Lake City. P.S.&T.
- Wooley, Jas., Salt Lake City. U.S.M.C.

Vermont
- Fountain, Joseph Harry, Burlington. 101st Am. Tr.
- Nason, Leonard, Norwich University. 76th F.A.
- Varnum, Guy, Barre. Ordnance.

Virginia
- Cocke, Francis, Roanoke. 217th Aero Sq.
- Isaid, James, Roanoke. 117th T.H. & M.P.
- Nei, D.D., Norfolk. U.S.N.R.F.
- Pallard, C., Richmond. 30th Eng.
- Pool, George, Norfolk, 111th F.A.
- Stuart, Wm. A., Big Stone Gap. 44th Art. Brig.
- Thompson, John, Petersburg. 248th Aero Sq.
- Trotter, Wm., Petersburg. U.S.N.R.F.
- Wallace, R.R., Hampton. 11th F.A.
- Wicker, John, Richmond. 499th Aero Sq.

Washington
- Fein, Fred, 1131 Pleasant St. U.S.N.R.F.
- Gordon, R.S., Spokane. 54th F.A.
- Johnson, Albert, Aberdeen. M.S.
- McDonald, C.B., Camp Lewis, Signal Corps.
- Moss, Harvey, Seattle. I.G.D.
- Redinger, Fred, Aberdeen. U.S.N.R.F.
- Sapp, C.S., Seattle. Ord.
- Shaw, Frederick, Tacoma. C.A.C.
- Simenton, Russ, Seattle. U.S.N.R.F.
- Sullivan, John, Seattle. M.I.B.
- Thompson, L.L., Olympia. U.S.N.R.F.

West Virginia
- Alderson, Fleming, Charleston. A.G.O.
- Arnold, Jackson, Weston. 150th Inf.
- Bond, John, 317 Michigan Ave. Gen. Staff 38th Div.
- Crockett, Joseph, Welch. 315th F.A.
- Davis, Richard, Morgantown. A.S.A.
- Ferguson, G.E., Charleston. 365th Inf.
- Godfrey, M.V., Charleston. Med. Corps.
- Jackson, Joseph, Charleston. 365th Inf.

- Jones, Clarence, Hinton. 8th Inf.
- McCamic, Charles, Wheeling. Ordn.
- Reass, Jos. H., Wheeling. Q.M.C.
- Shaw, Houston Geo., Wheeling. R.I.C.
- Simmons, W.J., Hinton. 40th Inf.
- Solins, Samuel, Welch. M.C.

Wisconsin
- Ackley, James, 417 Marston Ave., 168th Inf.
- Bellis, Newman, Wausau. 18th Inf.
- Chybowski, M.A., Milwaukee. M.O.T.C.
- Clarke, Robert H., La Crosse. Development Bn.
- Clow, Wm. K., Milwaukee. U.S.N.
- Crosby, H.S., Rhinelander.
- Cunningham, Rob., Janesville. Chemical Warfare.
- Davis, John, Milwaukee. Train. Cp.
- Dieterien, W.H., Milwaukee. 120th F.A.
- Dutscher, Geo., Milwaukee. F.A.C.O.T.S.
- Ferris, John, Milwaukee. Gen. Staff.
- Foster, Carlton, Oshkosh. 20th Eng.
- Lachenmaier, Fred, 312 Caswel Blk., 100th Div.
- Lee, Wilbur, Oconto. 127th Inf.
- Lystud, Andy, N. Hudson. 330th Mach. Gun.
- Merkel, Geo., Appleton. 127th Inf.
- Owens, Elmer, Milwaukee, 121st F.A.
- Pfeil, James, Milwaukee. 340th Inf.
- Prange, Herbert, Baraboo. 128th Inf.
- Salsman, John, Madison. 32d Div.
- Smith, B.L., Neenah. 18th Inf.
- Strampe, George, Janesville.
- Szultek, John, Milwaukee. 121st F.A.
- Witterstaffer, Walter, Milwaukee. 340th Inf.
- Woodworth, Leigh, Janesville.

Wyoming
- Dinneen, M.A., Cheyenne. 116th Amm. Tr.
- Gregg, Ben, Worland. 49th Reg.
- June, C.M., Cheyenne. 13th Div.
- McCarthy, D.C.M., Casper. U.S.N.
- Miller, L.A., Cheyenne. U.S.M.C.
- Powers, Ralph, Tarrington. 40th Inf.
- Shortell, William, Buffalo. 116th Am. Tr.
- Swenson, Nelsy, Douglas, 1st Inf.

World's War Veterans
- C.P. Dimmitt
- G.H.W. Rauschkolb

- Geo. E. David
- John S. Seibert
- Thomas H. Dempsey
- R.A. Thompson
- F.H. Rein
- Charles S. Watkins

Soldiers' And Sailors' Council
- S.M. Curtin

American Army Association
- H.W. Hillyer, 1215 Nat. Bank, Conwell Bldg., St. Louis, Co. B, 49 Mo. G.B.
- Louis R. Florin
- T.R. Smith, 2848 Lyon St., St. Louis, 11th Co. A., S.D., Garden City
- Joseph P. McGlinn
- J.A. Bernard, 706 Pearce Bldg., St. Louis. 45 U.S. Inf.
- Scott W. Lucas

www.ingramcontent.com/pod-product-compliance
Lightning Source LLC
Chambersburg PA
CBHW051829040426
42447CB00006B/438